GOOD MORNING,

GOD!

SPENDING TIME IN
HIS PRESENCE

Ginger Hurta

WESTBOW
PRESS®
A DIVISION OF THOMAS NELSON
& ZONDERVAN

Unless otherwise noted, all Scripture references in this book are taken from the NIV Version, copyright © 1985 by Zondervan Corporation. Used by permission of Zondervan Corporation, Hodder & Stroughton and Biblica.

WestBow Press books may be ordered through booksellers or by contacting:

WestBow Press
A Division of Thomas Nelson & Zondervan
1663 Liberty Drive
Bloomington, IN 47403
www.westbowpress.com
1 (866) 928-1240

ISBN: 978-1-5127-1358-9 (sc)
ISBN: 978-1-5127-1359-6 (hc)
ISBN: 978-1-5127-1357-2 (e)

Library of Congress Control Number: 2015915811

Print information available on the last page.

WestBow Press rev. date: 10/28/2015

This book is presented to:

_____

From:

_____

This book is dedicated to
the glory of God and to
my precious husband, Dennis.
He is the Angel God sent to me.

He is also the photographer
of the cover photo.

PREFACE

Several years ago the Lord called me to leave my job in the secular world and come to work for Him and care for His people. I have been incredibly blessed in doing so. Then He asked me to write a book for Him. As is my usual response to God's call, it takes me forever to process it. My first reaction is that He couldn't possibly be calling me or, how could He use me?

Praise God, through His grace, He has taught me that He isn't calling me personally to do these things, but that He wants to use me as His instrument to accomplish His work through me.

It is through my "quiet time" alone with Him each day that these things have been revealed to me. He placed in my heart that one of His greatest desires is for all of His children to spend time alone with him each day – time in His Word and in prayer.

Unfortunately, too many of us get so caught up in the busyness of the world that we "don't have time to spend time with Him." He impressed upon me to write this daily devotion in hopes that if people would just spend a few minutes each day with Him it would have a profound impact on their spiritual lives.

It has been an unimaginable blessing to spend time with Him as I prayed and asked the Holy Spirit to give me the scriptures and prayers God wants us to hear. I pray you will be richly blessed and your time with the Lord will become such a joy that you couldn't possibly start your day without first spending time with Him.

January

GOOD MORNING, GOD!
January 1

Lamentations 3:22-25

Because of the Lord's great love we are not consumed, for his compassions never fail. They are new every morning; great is your faithfulness. I say to myself, "The Lord is my portion; therefore I will wait for him. . ."

Good Morning, God! This is the time of new beginnings. It is a new year with all sorts of hopes and dreams. I am excited because this is an opportunity to begin afresh and make my life more of what You have planned for me before You laid the foundations of the earth! I am thankful that Your *compassions never fail. Great is Your faithfulness.* You are a glorious God of provision and mercy. Help me to be ever faithful to You. Let Your Spirit set me on fire for You.

Lord, let this new year be the one in which I . . .

GOOD MORNING, GOD!
January 2

Genesis 1:1-3

In the beginning God created the heavens and the earth. Now the earth was formless and empty, darkness was over the surface of the deep, and the Spirit of God was hovering over the waters. And God said, "Let there be light," and there was light.

Good Morning, God! How awesome are You, O Lord God Almighty, Your Glory is beyond the comprehension of my finite mind and yet, I see Your Majesty all around me. I am thankful to be a child of God. I have received this great inheritance through Your grace and goodness and the sacrifice of Your Precious Son. Praise be to the Father, Son and Holy Spirit.

Lord, I will praise You today by . . .

GOOD MORNING, GOD!
January 3

1Corinthians 13:4-7

Love is patient, love is kind. It does not envy, it does not boast, it is not proud. It is not rude, it is not self-seeking, it is not easily angered, it keeps no record of wrongs. Love does not delight in evil but rejoices with the truth. It always protects, always trusts, always hopes, always perseveres.

Good Morning, God! What a beautiful description of love. If only I could always keep these truths in my heart. These are truly the attributes of You, Father God. I strive each day to be more like Jesus. I want to show Your love in every action and word in my life. I want to be a reflection of Your love that shines so brightly it is blinding. I want others to know You as I know and love You.

Lord, show me how to be a better disciple so You can use me to . . .

GOOD MORNING, GOD!
January 4

Isaiah 64:8-9

Yet, O Lord, you are our Father. We are the clay, you are the potter; we are all the work of your hand. Do not be angry beyond measure, Lord; do not remember our sins forever. O, look on us, we pray, for we are all your people.

Good Morning, God! Lord, I pray that You make me and mold me into the creation You desire me to be. You are my Creator and I give my life to You—use me as You will. It is not my life, but my life in Christ that is important to Your Kingdom. Help me to further the Kingdom and lay myself aside for You. You have called me to be Your servant and it is my greatest joy.

Precious Savior, open my eyes to see . . .

GOOD MORNING, GOD!
January 5

Matthew 17:2, 5-7

There he was transfigured before them. His face shone like the sun, and his clothes became white as the light. . . . While he was speaking, a bright cloud enveloped them, and a voice from the cloud said, "This is my Son, whom I love; with him I am well pleased. Listen to him!"

Good Morning, God! What a wondrous sight – to see Christ in all His Glory and then to hear the very Words of God! *Listen to him!* Lord, I pray that I can hear Your voice as clearly as on that day when You spoke to the disciples. Let Your Words fill me with the desire to do Your will. Keep me so close to You that I can feel Your presence.

I love You, Lord and . . .

GOOD MORNING, GOD!
January 6

John 1:29-30

The next day John saw Jesus coming toward him and said, "Look, the Lamb of God, who takes away the sin of the world! This is the one I mean when I said, "A man who comes after me has surpassed me because he was before me."

Good Morning, God! Jesus, my Precious Savior, I love you, Lord. I am so thankful for Your sacrifice for me. I humble myself before You and give You worship and praise. I love spending time alone with You each day. I feel so close to You and it fills my day with joy and peace. I am ready to put on the *full armor of God* because You strengthen me. Send me forth to be Your servant. Guide me and direct my words and deeds. Let everything I do today bring You glory.

Help me to see as You see and . . .

GOOD MORNING, GOD!
January 7

Luke 15:18-20

"I will set out and go back to my father and say to him: 'Father, I have sinned against heaven and against you. I am no longer worthy to be called your son; make me like one of your hired men.'" So he got up and went to his father. But while he was still a long way off, his father saw him and was filled with compassion for him; he ran to his son, threw his arms around him and kissed him.

Good Morning, God! What a loving and compassionate God You are! Even when I turn my back on You and become completely degenerate, You are always waiting for me to return. You wait patiently and lovingly. I don't even have to run to You, You run to me the minute I repent. Thank You, Father God, for loving me so much. Thank You for Your forgiveness and grace. I love You, Lord.

Thank You, Lord, for . . .

GOOD MORNING, GOD!
January 8

James 4:13-15

"Today or tomorrow we will go to this or that city, spend a year there, carry on business and make money." Why, you do not even know what will happen tomorrow. What is your life? You are a mist that appears for a little while and then vanishes. Instead, you ought to say, "If it is the Lord's will, we will live and do this or that".

Good Morning, God! Isn't it just like me to have everything all planned out according to my terms and conditions? I'm sure everything must be up to me to be certain that things are done timely and correctly. I'll be sure everything is right. When I get so caught up in myself, I realize the folly I perpetrate. You are the Sovereign God and You reign. My life is merely a *mist and then vanishes.* I am thankful that You are the Lord of the universe and I can know my life will be according to Your will.

Lord, give me wisdom and patience to . . .

GOOD MORNING, GOD!
January 9

Psalm 108:1-4

My heart, O God, is steadfast; I will sing and make music with all my soul. Awake, harp and lyre! I will awaken the dawn. It will praise you, Lord, among the nations; I will sing of you among the peoples. How great is your love, higher than the heavens; your faithfulness reaches to the skies.

Good Morning, God! Lord, I love when I awaken and the first thing I think of is You. I love to just lie in bed each morning letting the sleep pass and the new day begin. What a joy it is to start each day thinking of You and Your goodness. You make my heart and soul sing Your praises. It is exciting to wait expectantly on what You have planned for me today. I am certain it will be wonderful for *great is your love, higher than the heavens; your faithfulness reaches to the skies.*

Lord, set me in motion this day to . . .

GOOD MORNING, GOD!
January 10

John 11:25-26

Jesus said to her, "I am the resurrection and the life. The one who believes in me will live, even though they die; and whoever lives by believing in me will never die. Do you believe this?" "Yes, Lord," she replied, "I believe that you are the Messiah, the Son of God, who is to come into the world."

Good Morning, God! This scripture is so very comforting. We all know we will lose loved ones and our hearts will be broken when that time comes. Because of Your deep love and grace, You prepare us for these times with Your promises of eternal life. *You are the resurrection and the life.* I do, believe, Lord. I know that You are *the Messiah, the Son of God, who is to come into the world.*

Thank You for Your promises that comfort us. Help me to . . .

GOOD MORNING, GOD!
January 11

James 5:10-11

Brothers and sisters, as an example of patience in the face of suffering, take the prophets who spoke in the name of the Lord. As you know, we count as blessed those who have persevered. You have heard of Job's perseverance and have seen what the Lord finally brought about. The Lord is full of compassion and mercy.

Good Morning, God! Patience is definitely a virtue I am lacking. It is so hard to be patient *in the face of suffering.* It seems that I must do something to make things right. Lord, help me to remember that it isn't up to me but to You. Help me to wait on You and know that in You is the victory! Teach me the perseverance of Job because I know You are *full of compassion and mercy.*

Lord, bless me to persevere so that . . .

GOOD MORNING, GOD!
January 12

Psalm 113:1-5

Praise the Lord. Praise the Lord, you his servants; praise the name of the Lord. Let the name of the Lord be praised, both now and forevermore. From the rising of the sun to the place where it sets, the name of the Lord is to be praised. The Lord is exalted over all the nations, his glory above the heavens. Who is like the Lord our God, the One who sits enthroned on high . . .?

Good Morning, God! I love to start the day in the Psalms. Your servant, David, had such a close, personal relationship with You. He truly knew You and loved You. He turned to You for guidance and for Your help in every situation. David gives me hope because even though he *was a man after Your own heart*, he was also a sinner. Reading the beauty of his words gives me the hope of forgiveness and a closer relationship with You.

Lord, forgive me of my sins and let me *praise the name of the Lord* by . . .

GOOD MORNING, GOD!
January 13

John 21:4-6

Early in the morning, Jesus stood on the shore, but the disciples did not realize that it was Jesus. He called out to them, "Friends, haven't you any fish?" "No," they answered. He said, "Throw your net on the right side of the boat and you will find some." When they did, they were unable to haul the net in because of the large number of fish.

Good Morning, God! This scripture speaks to profoundly to me. I am continually "fishing" and don't seem to be making progress. I am so busy trying to do Your work on my own initiative. I get so caught up trying to fix things that I don't have time to pray or spend time with You. Lord, let me always know that when I go to You first You will solve my problems – not only solve them, but give me so much more than I could ever ask. You make everything right to the point of overflowing.

Lord, help me to seek Your guidance for . . .

GOOD MORNING, GOD!
January 14

Acts 3:6-9

    Then Peter said, "Silver or gold I do not have, but what I do have I give you. In the name of Jesus Christ of Nazareth, walk." Taking him by the right hand, he helped him up, and instantly the man's feet and ankles became strong. He jumped to his feet and began to walk. Then he went with them into the temple courts, walking and jumping, and praising God.

    Good Morning, God! What an awesome scripture. So many times we ask You for what we think is our ultimate need and in return You give us more than we could ever imagine. I doubt that this lame man could even conceive the possibility of being healed. He only hoped for a few coins to sustain him for a moment. You healed him completely and made him whole. In Your goodness and grace, You used Your disciple, Peter, to perform a miracle for this man.

    Lord, let me expect miracles in order to . . .

GOOD MORNING, GOD!
January 15

Titus 2: 6-8

    Similarly, encourage the young men to be self-controlled. In everything set them an example by doing what is good. In your teachings show integrity, seriousness and soundness of speech that cannot be condemned, so that those who oppose you may be ashamed because they have nothing bad to say about us.

    Good Morning, God! We have all heard a child mimic something we just said – and usually word-for-word. We don't realize how each word and action is being absorbed by someone, hopefully for the good, but not always. Help me to be ever mindful of the fact that everything about me is a reflection of You because I am Your child. Help me to be aware that others are not only judging what I do personally, but they are judging You because they know I am a Christian. Let me be a shining example of You in all that I do.

    Help me to glorify You today by . ..

GOOD MORNING, GOD!
January 16

Amos 9:11-12

"In that day I will restore David's fallen tent. I will repair its broken places, restore its ruins, and build it as it used to be, so that they may possess the remnant of Edom and all the nations that bear my name," declares the Lord, who will do these things.

Good Morning, God! Your Words of promise to the Jewish Nation are glorious. They have been in exile and suffering for thousands of years. What comfort it must be for them to read these Words. You are a God of promise. You will keep Your covenant with Abraham and David. Our Savior will reign in Your land forever. The enemies of Israel will be crushed and will bow to the Messiah they rejected. Praise God from Whom all blessings flow.

Lord, let me bless Israel as You command and . . .

GOOD MORNING, GOD!
January 17

Romans 13:11-12

And do this, understanding the present time. The hour has come for you to wake up from your slumber, because our salvation is nearer now than when we first believed. The night is nearly over; the day is almost here. So let us put aside the deeds of darkness and put on the armor of light.

Good Morning, God! Lord, I know You can return at any time – *as a thief in the night.* Help me to overcome my complacency and be ready. Let me *put aside the deeds of darkness and put on the armor of light.* Give me the words and the courage to proclaim Jesus Christ to every unbeliever with whom I come in contact. *The night is nearly over* and I don't want to leave anyone behind. You have commanded me *to go and make disciples.*

Lord, set someone in my path today so that I can tell them of You and . . .

GOOD MORNING, GOD!
January 18

James 15:13-16

Is any one of you in trouble? He should pray. Is anyone happy? Let him sings songs of praise. Is any one of you sick? He should call the elders of the church to pray over him and anoint him with oil in the name of the Lord. And the prayer offered in faith will make the sick person well; the Lord will raise him up if he has sinned, he will be forgiven. Therefore confess your sins to each other and pray for each other so that you may be healed. The prayer of a righteous man is powerful and effective.

Good Morning, God! Lord, You have given me Your Spirit by which to pray and unleash the power of prayer. You tell me that *the prayer of a righteous man is powerful and effective.* Let me claim that power for Your glory. Give me the faith to pray in anticipation of You answering my prayers. You are a mighty and gracious God.

Teach me to pray with the power of the Holy Spirit and . . .

GOOD MORNING, GOD!
January 19

Revelation 5:11-12

Then I looked and heard the voice of many angels, numbering thousands upon thousands, and ten thousand times ten thousand. They encircle the throne and the living creatures and the elders. In a loud voice they sang: "Worthy is the Lamb who was slain, to receive power and wealth and wisdom and strength and honor and glory and praise?"

Good Morning, God! O God, what a sight that will be when I stand before Your throne and sing Your praises with the multitudes. I can't imagine the beautiful music of all those voices. All glory, praise and honor are Yours, Lord. I want to be in that number and sing Your praises forever more. *Worthy is the Lamb who was slain.* Thanks be to God.

Lord, I praise You and . . .

GOOD MORNING, GOD!
January 20

Isaiah 33:5-6

The Lord is exalted, for he dwells on high; he will fill Zion with justice and righteousness. He will be the sure foundation for your times, a rich store of salvation and wisdom and knowledge; the fear of the Lord is the key to this treasure.

Good Morning, God! Come, Lord Jesus, come. Let the earth be filled with your *justice and righteousness.* In these times, it seems we have fallen so far away from You and Your ways. We have made a mockery of the judicial system; what is wrong is right and what is right is wrong. Be our *sure foundation.* Let us return to You with *the fear of the Lord.* Let us seek You in all we do to do Your will.

Lord I exalt You and . . .

GOOD MORNING, GOD!
January 21

Proverbs 4:20-22

My son, pay attention to what I say; listen closely to my words. Do not let them out of your sight, keep them within your heart; for they are life to those who find them and health to a man's whole body.

Good Morning, God! Lord, I love to spend time in Your Word each morning. I want to *keep them within my heart.* I want to dwell on them and hear the message You have for me. This is my opportunity to know Your heart, O God. You reveal Yourself to me through the scripture. You reveal the plans You have for me. Let my heart and mind be open to every Word from You. Let me take them forth to further Your Kingdom.

Lord, let me *listen* today and . . .

GOOD MORNING, GOD!
January 22

1 Kings 17:13-14

Elijah said to her, "Don't be afraid. Go home and do as you have said. But first make a small cake of bread for me from what you have and bring it to me, and then make something for yourself and your son. For this is what the Lord, the God of Israel, says: 'The jar of flour will not be used up and the jug of oil will not run dry until the day the Lord gives rain on the land.'"

Good Morning, God! Lord, Your promises are sweeter than honey. Your Word fills me with all the nourishment I need to sustain me. Give me the faith of the woman in this story. Let me completely give my life to You, for I know Your mercies endure forever. You are the Lord who provides for Your children. Praise God!

Lord, give me the trust to . . .

GOOD MORNING, GOD!
January 23

Psalm 46:1-4

God is our refuge and strength, an ever-present help in trouble. Therefore we will not fear, though the earth give way and the mountains fall into the heart of the sea, its waters roar and foam and the mountains quake with their surging. There is a river whose streams make glad the city of God, the holy place where the Most High dwells.

Good Morning, God! Even though I've heard these verses since I was a child, I hear them afresh today. You are such a Mighty God – *our refuge and strength, an ever-present help in trouble.* Lord, let me completely give my life to You for safe-keeping. I will rest in Your arms even when the *mountains quake.* I am comforted and secure in Your love. You are the Most High and You promise to take care of me. What can I fear?

Lord, thank You for always being there for me even when . . .

GOOD MORNING, GOD!
January 24

Exodus 17:4-6a

Then Moses cried out to the Lord, "What am I to do with these people? They are almost ready to stone me." The Lord answered Moses, "Go out in front of the people. Take with you some of the elders of Israel and take in your hand the staff with which you struck the Nile and go. I will stand there before you by the rock at Horeb. Strike the rock, and water will come out of it for the people to drink."

Good Morning, God! Sometimes when it seems things can't get any worse, they do. Moses is dealing with the grumblings of the Israelites and now *they are ready to stone him.* Moses knew what to do in this circumstance – he *cried out to the Lord.* I love where You say that *I will stand there before you by the rock.* When I cry out to You, O Lord, You are always there for me. No matter my needs at the time, You will provide.

Help me to not despair today but to call on You to . . .

GOOD MORNING, GOD!
January 25

Ephesians 2:19b-22

. . . but fellow citizens of God's people and also members of his household built on the foundation of the apostles and prophets, with Christ Jesus himself as the chief cornerstone. In him the whole building is joined together and rises to become a holy temple in the Lord. And in him you too are being built together to become a dwelling in which God lives by his Spirit.

Good Morning, God! What a blessing to be a part of the Body of Christ. Your Church is built on the *foundation of the apostles and prophets, with Christ Jesus himself as the chief cornerstone.* You have called me to be Your disciple, joined together with Christ to further the Kingdom. Your Spirit dwells within me. You are my rock and my salvation. I give You praise and worship.

Put me to work for You today to . . .

GOOD MORNING, GOD!
January 26

Psalm 46:10-11

He says, "Be still, and know that I am God; I will be exalted among the nations, will be exalted in the earth." The Lord Almighty is with us; the God of Jacob is our fortress.

Good Morning, God! This sounds so simple, just *be still and know that I am God*. Of course, I can do that. You are God alone. I see Your handiwork all around me. I love You and worship You, but what do I do when the waves come crashing in all around me? What do I do when everything seems lost? I must turn to You, O God. Give me the wisdom and courage to *be still*. You promise to never leave me or forsake me. Let me cling to that thought and have the faith and trust to give all my cares to You. Your mighty hands will lift me up on eagle's wings.

Lord, You are my fortress. Help me to . . .

GOOD MORNING, GOD!
January 27

Ephesians 6:10-12

Finally, be strong in the Lord and in his mighty power. Put on the full armor of God, so that you can take your stand against the devil's schemes. For our struggle is not against flesh and blood, but against the rulers, against the authorities, against the powers of this dark world and against the spiritual forces of evil in the heavenly realms.

Good Morning, God! I believe one of the devil's greatest schemes is to convince the world that he does not exist. He uses the ploy that there is no supernatural and therefore, no devil. Your Word is very explicit in warning *against the spiritual forces of evil in the heavenly realms*. Satan was made prince of darkness when sin entered the world. Make me ever aware of his presence. Let Your Spirit fill me and give me the strength to resist temptation.

Help me to *be strong in the Lord and his mighty power* to overcome . . .

GOOD MORNING, GOD!
January 28

Colossians 4:2-6

Devote yourselves to prayer, being watchful and thankful. And pray for us too, that God may open a door for our message, so that we may proclaim the mystery of Christ, for which I am an ambassador in chains. Pray that I may proclaim it clearly, as I should. Be wise in the way you act toward outsiders; make the most of every opportunity. Let your conversation be always full of grace, seasoned with salt, so that you may know how to answer everyone.

Good Morning, God! I love spending time with You in prayer – my source of revival in the morning. I know that Paul prayed in the Spirit and completely gave his life for You -- *for which I am an ambassador in chains.* He would even preach the Good News to his guards. Help me to *be wise in the way I act toward outsiders.* Help me see everyone through Your eyes. *Let my conversation be always full of grace, seasoned with salt, so that I may know how to answer everyone.* Help me to be bold and brave for You.

Lord, give me the words to . . .

GOOD MORNING, GOD!
January 29

Psalm 43:2-4

With your hand you drove out the nations and planted our ancestors; you crushed the peoples and made our ancestors flourish. It was not by their sword that they won the land, nor did their arm bring them victory; it was your right hand, your arm, and the light of your face, for you loved them. You are my King and my God who decrees victories to Jacob.

Good Morning, God! You know, Lord, that when I read scriptures like this that You are *the God who decree victories to Jacob,* it is hard for me to conceive that You are speaking to me. I know Jacob was Your chosen one to establish the Twelve Tribes of Israel. I am so insignificant I can't relate to such grandeur. And yet, I know that every Word is given for me. It is not what I can do, but what You can do through me. I can't do anything on my own, but, with Your strength, I'm strong.

Lord, let Your strength flow through me so that . . .

GOOD MORNING, GOD!
January 30

James 5:17-20

Elijah was a human being, even as we are. He prayed earnestly that it would not rain, and it did not rain on the land for three and a half years. Again he prayed, and the heavens gave rain, and the earth produced its crops. My brothers and sisters, if one of you should wander from the truth and someone should bring that person back, remember this: Whoever turns a sinner from the error of their way will save them from death and cover over a multitude of sins.

Good Morning, God! Lord, You tell me over and over again of the power of prayer. Prayer unleashes the Power of the Holy Spirit through me. Let my prayers be fervent and true. Don't let my mind wander but be totally engulfed in You and Your will for my life. I pray for Your will to be done in my life and through me. I thank You that I know You hear my prayers.

Lord, let me have the faith of Elijah when I pray so that . . .

GOOD MORNING, GOD!
January 31

Psalm 89:1-2

I will sing of the Lord's great love forever; with my mouth I will make your faithfulness known through all generations. I will declare that your love stands firm forever, that you have established your faithfulness in heaven itself.

Good Morning, God! Lord, it is so obvious that all the Christian song writers draw their music from the scriptures. I love the song that *sings of the Lord's great love forever.* I am so filled with Your love right now – filled to the point my heart is overflowing. It is such a soothing thought to imagine that Your love lasts forever. I can rest in that thought in the midst of whatever Satan attempts to deceive me with today. I am a child of the Most High God. *You have established your faithfulness in heaven itself,* and I know You are holding me and keeping me safe. Thank You, Jesus.

Help me to glorify You today by . .

∗ ✠ ∗

February

GOOD MORNING, GOD!
February 1

Joshua 3:14-16a

So when the people broke camp to cross the Jordan, the priests carrying the Ark of the Covenant went ahead of them. Now the Jordan is at flood stage all during harvest. Yet as soon as the priests who carried the ark reached the Jordan and their feet touched the water's edge, the water from upstream stopped flowing. It piled up in a heap a great distance away.

Good Morning, God! Lord, how can I ever doubt You? How can I imagine that I have problems too big for You to handle? There is nothing in the world more important than knowing You and that You reign. Even when things seem impossible and out of control, You reign. You reign to the heights of the mountains to the depths of the sea. This is the world You created and it will continue in Your order forever. If ever I question Your power, let me recall this verse.

I love You, Lord, and . . .

GOOD MORNING, GOD!
February 2

Matthew 6:19-21

"*Do not store up for yourselves treasures on earth, where moths and vermin destroy, and where thieves break in and steal. But store up for yourselves treasures in heaven, where moths and vermin do not destroy, and where thieves do not break in and steal. For where your treasure is, there you heart will be also.*"

Good Morning, God! Lord, why do we spend so much of our time and energy in an attempt to gain great wealth when the only thing that matters is You and Your Kingdom? What a tragedy that so many parents work long hours to have the money to buy their children the things they want, when all they really want is time with their parents? Lord, we've got it all backwards. Help me to place the most value on the things above. Forgive me for being so materialistic and trying to keep up with the world.

Set my heart on the path of doing Your will to . . .

GOOD MORNING, GOD!
February 3

Psalm 139:1-6

You have searched me, Lord, and you know me. You know when I sit and when I rise; you perceive my thoughts from afar. You discern my going out and my lying down; you are familiar with all my ways. Before a word is on my tongue you, Lord, know it completely. You hem me in behind and before, and you lay your hand upon me. Such knowledge is too wonderful for me, too lofty for me to attain.

Good Morning, God! Lord, *you perceive my thoughts from afar.* That can be very disturbing when I know all my thoughts are not what You would have them be. I am filled with pride, deceit, prejudice, and even sometimes malice, but I think no one knows but me. How foolish I am. *Before a word is on my tongue you, Lord, know it completely.* You are a loving and forgiving God. *You lay Your hand upon me.* You know my greatest desire is to do what is right. I just fall way short at times.

Thank You for loving me and . . .

GOOD MORNING, GOD!
February 4

1 Kings 18:37-39

Answer me, Lord, answer me, so these people will know that you, Lord, are God, and that you are turning their hearts back again. Then the fire of the Lord fell and burned up the sacrifice, the wood, the stones and the soil, and also licked up the water in the trench. When all the people saw this, they fell prostrate and cried, "The Lord – he is God! The Lord – he is God!"

Good Morning, God! Elijah was a mighty and faithful prophet for You, O Lord. When he prayed, You gave him astounding results. I love that he asked *Lord, answer me, so these people will know that you, Lord, are God.* He was not worried about his standing before these people, only Yours. When the people saw the display of Your power, *they fell prostrate and cried, "The Lord – he is God!"* Praise God for men like Elijah who were completely devoted to You. Help me to have that faith.

Lord, let me pray with the faith of Elijah so that . . .

GOOD MORNING, GOD!
February 5

Acts 4:12-14

". . . Salvation is found in no one else, for there is no other name under heaven given to mankind by which we must be saved." When they saw the courage of Peter and John and realized that they were unschooled, ordinary men, they were astonished and they took note that these men and been with Jesus. But since they could see the man who had been healed standing there with them, there was nothing they could say.

Good Morning, God! O Lord, how powerful is Your Holy Spirit. These *unschooled, ordinary men* had just performed a miracle in Your name and made a lame man walk. I love the fact that You use each of us to perform Your miracles – not just the people who are Bible scholars and ministers. When we accept Jesus Christ as our Savior, we are indwelt with the Holy Spirit – not just the Spirit but the Power of that Spirit. Let me feel and use that Power for Your glory.

Let people see that I have been with Jesus and I have His Power to . . .

GOOD MORNING, GOD!
February 6

Numbers 6:24-26

"The Lord bless you and keep you; the Lord make his face shine on you and be gracious to you; the Lord turn his face toward you and give you peace."

Good Morning, God! Lord, these words of Scripture are absolutely beautiful. I feel cocooned in Your divine presence and goodness to me. I am overwhelmed by Your love and mercy. I realize I am showered with these promises every hour of every day. I am surrounded by the *light of Your face* and You are truly *gracious to me.* Not only that, but you *give Your peace* to me. Your peace is so precious. You are a Mighty and Loving God. I give You praise and glory forever.

Lord, let me use this blessing to bless others by . . .

GOOD MORNING, GOD!
February 7

Acts 5:27-29

The apostles were brought in and made to appear before the Sanhedrin to be questioned by the high priests. "We gave you strict orders not to teach in this name," he said. "Yet you have filled Jerusalem with your teaching and are determined to make us guilty of this man's blood." Peter and the other apostles replied: "We must obey God rather than human beings!"

Good Morning, God! O, Lord, I wish I had this much courage when put on trial for my faith. Peter was so sure he was doing Your will that it never occurred to him to be worried about what might happen to him. He only wanted to *fill Jerusalem with your teaching.* Lord, You know this is my desire. You know my heart and You know I love You. Help me to strengthen my faith and not be afraid to speak out for You.

Help me to *obey God rather than human beings* when . . .

GOOD MORNING, GOD!
February 8

Philippians 2:6-8

Who, being in very nature God, did not consider equality with God something to be used to his own advantage; rather, he made himself nothing by taking the very nature of a servant, being made in human likeness. And being found in appearance as a man, he humbled himself by becoming obedient to death – even death on a cross.

Good Morning, God! What a glorious Savior we have. Thank You, Jesus, for leaving the splendor and beauty of heaven to come to this earth just for me. It is so hard to fathom the reality of the King of the universe, the Lord Almighty giving Himself to die on the cross for me – one of the world's worst sinners. Your love and grace are truly amazing. I long to be Your servant.

Lord, teach me humility today to . . .

GOOD MORNING, GOD!
February 9

Philippians 2:9-11

Therefore God exalted him to the highest place and gave him the name that is above every name, that at the name of Jesus every knee should bow, in heaven and on earth and under the earth, and every tongue confess that Jesus Christ is Lord, to the glory of God the Father.

Good Morning, God! With all the world religions we now have and all the conflicts within them, what a mess we have created. We have world powers working to overcome weaker nations. We have powerful people attempting to overcome those less fortunate. What a beautiful day it will be when our Lord Jesus Christ appears in the heavens with the sound of a trumpet and riding on a white horse. And then, truly *every tongue will confess that Jesus Christ is Lord, to the glory of God the Father.*

Lord, I give You all the glory and honor. Thank you for . . .

GOOD MORNING, GOD!
February 10

Luke 12:11-12

[Jesus speaking to His disciples. . .] "When you are brought before synagogues, rulers and authorities, do not worry about how you will defend yourselves, or what you will say, for the Holy Spirit will teach you at that time what you should say."

Good Morning, God! There are so many times I know You are calling me to witness to someone. I can feel You tugging at me and yet too many times I shrug it off as not real. How can I be so foolish? You tell me that even if I am *brought before synagogues, rulers and authorities, do not worry about how* I will defend myself. Somehow, witnessing to a friend doesn't seem to fall into that category and yet I'm afraid or embarrassed that I will say the wrong thing. Your Spirit will give me the words.

Lord, give me the wisdom and courage to . . .

GOOD MORNING, GOD!
February 11

Genesis 50:19-21

But Joseph said to them, "Don't be afraid. Am I in the place of God? You intended to harm me, but God intended it for good to accomplish what is now being done, the saving of many lives. So then, don't be afraid. I will provide for you and your children." And he assured them and spoke kindly to them.

Good Morning, God! Lord, it is a blessing that we can't see the big picture. You alone are God and You alone know the future. When things don't seem as they should and even seem out of control, Your Mighty Hand is orchestrating the entire universe. We simply have to pray and wait on the Lord. In Your infinite wisdom, all things will be made right. You hold our lives in the Palm of Your Hand. All praise and glory and honor to You, our Lord and King.

Lord, give me the wisdom to wait on You and . . .

GOOD MORNING, GOD!
February 12

1 Corinthians 15:55-58

"Where, O death, is your victory? Where, O death, is your sting? The sting of death is sin, and the power of sin is the law. But thanks be to God! He gives us the victory through our Lord Jesus Christ. Therefore, my dear brothers and sisters, stand firm. Let nothing move you. Always give yourselves fully to the work of the Lord, because you know that your labor in the Lord is not in vain.

Good Morning, God! Lord, as I go about my day, let me *stand firm* in the knowledge that You reign. You have planned my day even before I arose. You have planned my life to Your purpose and glory. I want to *give myself fully to the work of the Lord*. I want to share the Good News of Your love and mercy. *Let nothing move me.* You have overcome the *sting of death* by Your sacrifice on the cross that we may spend eternity with You. *Thanks be to God!*

Lord, guide my path today in order to . . .

GOOD MORNING, GOD!
February 13

Galatians 6:7-10

Do not be deceived: God cannot be mocked. A man reaps what he sows. Whoever sows to please their flesh, from the flesh will reap destruction; whoever sows to please the Spirit, from the Spirit will reap eternal life. Let us not become weary in doing good, for at the proper time we will reap a harvest if we do not give up. Therefore, as we have opportunity, let us do good to all people, especially to those who belong to the family of believers.

Good Morning, God! How many times have I quoted this scripture? It is evident in the law of nature that one reaps what he sows. Apple trees do not produce oranges. I need to spend more time in Your Word to light my path. It is so easy to lolly-gag along thinking I'm doing what is right while I am pleasing myself. Sometimes it just feels good. Give me wisdom to please the Spirit and not the flesh. Help me to *not give up* and follow the leading of Your Spirit.

Guide me *to do good to all people* and . . .

GOOD MORNING, GOD!
February 14

Joshua 6:20-21a

When the trumpets sounded, the army shouted, and at the sound of the trumpet, when the men gave a loud shout, the wall collapsed; so everyone charged straight in, and they took the city. They devoted the city to the Lord. . .

Good Morning, God! This is such a familiar Bible story of Joshua and the Israelites in the battle of Jericho. I learned it as a child and believe it with my whole heart. I am thankful my mother took me to Sunday School and church and gave me a firm faith foundation. It grieves me to think of the people who read this and don't believe it is possible and don't understand that You set the world in motion according to Your plan for our salvation and Your glory. Thanks be to God!

Lord, let me devote myself to You and . . .

GOOD MORNING, GOD!
February 15

Psalm 91:1-4

Whoever dwells in the shelter of the Most High will rest in the shadow of the Almighty. I will say of the Lord, "He is my refuge and my fortress, my God, in whom I trust." Surely he will save you from the fowler's snare and from the deadly pestilence. He will cover you with his feathers, and under his wings you will find refuge; his faithfulness will be your shield and rampart.

Good Morning, God! I feel Your unending love and comfort in these words. Every word is overflowing with an artist's masterpiece of Who You are. You are *the Most High, the Almighty, my refuge and fortress.* Not only do I have nothing to fear, but I can rest assured that you *save me from the fowler's snare and from the deadly pestilence.* I am safe and secure and, *under his wings I will find refuge.* I want to dwell in *the shelter of the Most High* forever. It will be my sanctuary shared with You. I have nothing to fear.

Thank You for Your faithfulness, O God, and . . .

GOOD MORNING, GOD!
February 16

Mark 11: 22-24

"Have faith in God," Jesus answered. "Truly I tell you, if anyone says to this mountain, 'Go, throw yourself into the sea, and does not doubt in their heart but believes that what they say will happen, it will be done for them.' Therefore I tell you, whatever you ask for in prayer, believe that you have received it, and it will be yours."

Good Morning, God! It seems this scripture is often misunderstood. It pictures You as Santa Clause or a bell hop and this is not true. I believe You are telling me that if I pray with complete faith that my prayers will be answered. *With You all things are possible.* If I pray for things that are in Your will and believe, *it will be mine.* You alone see the tapestry from the top and what is best for Your children. My prayers will be answered according to Your will and not whether or not I have enough faith. I do have enough faith and I trust You to answer my prayers.

Teach me to pray with faith and . . .

GOOD MORNING, GOD!
February 17

Isaiah 43:18-20

"Forget the former things; do not dwell on the past. See, I am doing a new thing! Now it springs up; do you not perceive it? I am making a way in the wilderness and streams in the wasteland."

Good Morning, God! O God of love and promises, I can't possibly dwell in the past or even on anything that troubles me when I read Your Word. You fill it with promises of hope and joy. You know that Your people can't fully comprehend the magnitude of Your love and Majesty, so You give us these words to lift us up and strengthen us. *You are continually doing a new thing* in my life. You open doors of opportunity and mercies each day; *do you not perceive it?* How glorious. Thank You, Lord.

Lord, let me see Your wonders with a new eye today and . . .

GOOD MORNING, GOD!
February 18

1 Corinthians 12:7-9

Now to each one the manifestation of the Spirit is given for the common good. To one there is given through the Spirit a message of wisdom, to another a message of knowledge by means of the same Spirit, to another faith by the same Spirit, to another gifts of healing by that one Spirit.

Good Morning, God! You tell us again and again that we have all been given gifts of the Spirit to be used for Your glory. I pray that I have the faith and wisdom to discern my gifts and put them to the use of furthering Your Kingdom. Let me know the power of the Holy Spirit that dwells within me and use that power for Your good. Don't let me believe Satan's lies that I am not worthy to be used by You. I am filled with gifts of the Spirit that You designed specifically for me. Let me be Your servant.

Thank You for loving me enough to fill me with Your Spirit and let me . . .

GOOD MORNING, GOD!
February 19

Matthew 18:21-22

Then Peter came to Jesus and asked, "Lord, how many times shall I forgive my brother or sister who sins against me? Up to seven times?" Jesus answered, "I tell you, not seven times, but seventy-seven times."

Good Morning, God! Lord, You know this is really a hard scripture to follow. When I am angry or hurt my first instinct is to lash back. Also, You don't mention anything about the person apologizing or asking for forgiveness. I also know You are not asking me to become a "doormat" but to have the heart of Christ. When I think of the forgiveness You shower upon me, how can I not forgive? When I think of Your love and mercy to me, one of the world's foremost sinners, how can I not show love and mercy to others?

Lord, teach me to forgive as You forgive and . . .

GOOD MORNING, GOD!
February 20

Mark 4:21-23

He said to them, "Do you bring in a lamp to put it under a bowl or a bed? Instead, don't you put it on its stand? For whatever is hidden is meant to be disclosed, and whatever is concealed is meant to be brought out into the open. If anyone has ears to hear, let them hear."

Good Morning, God! Lord, You know my deepest desire is for others to see Your light in me and to know You. I pray that Your Spirit burns so brightly in me that I can shine Your light all around. It is not what I do, but what You do through me. Let me be a vessel of Your Light. Use me to be a beacon to light the path for others to come to You. Let Your Light shine brightly through me and that I bring You glory. It's all to Your glory, O Lord.

Lord, use me today to . . .

GOOD MORNING, GOD!
February 21

Psalm 16:7-9

I will praise the Lord, who counsels me; even at night my heart instructs me. I keep my eyes always on the Lord. With him at my right hand, I will not be shaken. Therefore my heart is glad and my tongue rejoices; my body also will rest secure.

Good Morning, God! It is no wonder that 'David was a man after Your own Heart.' He truly knew You and relied on You for his very life. Lord, I want to know You better and love You more. I want to be as close to You as David was. I know You are *at my right hand and I will not be shaken.* You will be with me always and *my heart is glad and my tongue rejoices.* I have nothing to fear. *My body also will rest secure.* I know You will be with me until the end of the age. Praise God!

Lord, let me sing Your praises today by . . .

GOOD MORNING, GOD!
February 22

Luke 6:35-36

But love your enemies, do good to them, and lend to them without expecting to get anything back. Then your reward will be great, and you will be children of the Most High, because he is kind to the ungrateful and wicked. Be merciful, just as your Father is merciful.

Good Morning, God! Lord, I know You say to *love your enemies*, but that isn't always easy. I know with Your help and guidance I can do this. I want to be merciful as You are merciful. I want my heart to be compassionate as You are compassionate. I want to love as You love. I want to forgive as You forgive. Lord, remove my pride and let me be more like You. Let me see with Your eyes. Let me be Your hands and feet in a hurting world and I will give You all the glory.

Lord, as a *child of the Most High*, help me to . . .

GOOD MORNING, GOD!
February 23

Ephesians 3:11-15

So Christ himself gave the apostles, the prophets, the evangelists, the pastors and teachers, to equip his people for works of service, so that the body of Christ may be built up until we all reach unity in the faith and in the knowledge of the Son of God and become mature, attaining to the whole measure of the fullness of Christ.

Good Morning, God! Lord, I know You are continually working within me to bring me closer to You and to a greater understanding of Your Word. I give You thanks and praise for this. You not only call us, but equip us to do Your work. Through You all things are possible. Help me to *reach unity in the faith and knowledge of the Son of God*. Help me to *build up the body of Christ*. Give me Your wisdom and passion to set the world on fire for You so that we can *attain the whole measure of the fullness of Christ*.

Lord, inspire me to . . .

GOOD MORNING, GOD!
February 24

Romans 23:21-23

But now apart from the law the righteousness of God has been made known, to which the Law and the Prophets testify. This righteousness is given through faith in Jesus Christ to all who believe. There is no difference between Jew and Gentile, for all have sinned and fall short of the glory of God and all are justified freely by his grace through the redemption that came by Christ Jesus.

Good Morning, God! Lord, how comforting are these words. *For all have sinned and fall short of the glory of God.* No matter how hard I try, I can never not sin. I try and pray and turn right around and do the same things over again. Please forgive me, Precious Savior. I know when I repent You continue to forgive me because I am *justified freely by Your grace.* You died for me that I might be set free from the bondage of sin. Thank You, Lord Jesus.

Lord, let me show Your grace to others today by . . .

GOOD MORNING, GOD!
February 25

Psalm 104:1-3

Praise the Lord, O my soul. O Lord my God, you are very great; you are clothed with splendor and majesty. He wraps himself in light as with a garment; he stretches out the heavens like a tent and lays the beams of his upper chambers on their waters. He makes the clouds his chariot and rides on the wings of the wind.

Good Morning, God! *Praise the Lord, O my soul,* indeed. What a beautiful picture of You, my God and King. I can't begin to imagine Your Majesty. My feeble human mind is incapable of comprehending how awesome You are. I would love to be like Moses and hide in the cleft of the rock and have You show me a glimpse of Your Glory. I love You, Lord, and I give You all my praise and worship. You alone are God. Thank You for loving someone as insignificant as me.

Mighty God, show me Your Glory and . . .

GOOD MORNING, GOD!
February 26

Proverbs 30:7-9

Two things I ask of you, O Lord; do not refuse me before I die: Keep falsehood and lies far from me; give me neither poverty nor riches, but give me only my daily bread. Otherwise, I may become poor and steal, and so dishonor the name of my God.

Good Morning, God! Oh my goodness, Lord, You did give Solomon wisdom. Who but a wise man blessed by God could pray such a prayer? It is so simple and yet profound. Falsehood can destroy our life. It can destroy our relationships and bring us to ruin. It can delude us and keep us from a relationship with You. All we truly need is our *daily bread.* You provide all that we need each day. Help me to see that and not long for more. I have all I need in You. Praise God from Whom all blessings flow.

Lord, give me wisdom to . . .

GOOD MORNING, GOD!
February 27

Romans 6:22-23

But now that you have been set free from sin and have become slaves to God, the benefit you reap leads to holiness, and the result is eternal life. For the wages of sin is death, but the gift of God is eternal life in Christ Jesus our Lord.

Good Morning, God! Lord, I know my sin pulls me away from You. You do not move, but when I know I am doing wrong, I feel You are far away. I realize it is me and my actions that drive a wedge between us. I am happy to be a *slave to You, O God.* Because You have *set me free from sin,* I now can be Your child and receive *the gift of God which is eternal life in Christ Jesus our Lord.* Thank You, Jesus, for dying for me. I love You, Lord.

Lord, help me to draw closer to You so that . . .

GOOD MORNING, GOD!
February 28

John 21:17

The third time he said to him, "Simon son of John, do you love me?" Peter was hurt because Jesus asked him the third time, "Do you love me?" He said, "Lord, you know all things; you know that I love you." Jesus, said, "Feed my sheep."

Good Morning, God! Lord, I love this scripture. As You predicted, Peter denied You three times. In one of Your final visits with the disciples after Your resurrection, You give Peter a chance to vindicate himself. You love Peter and know the plans You have for him. You give us all a chance to vindicate ourselves. I, like Peter, have denied You at some point in my life. Yet You want me to *Feed Your sheep.* I am so thankful You are a merciful and forgiving Savior. I am thankful You *know all things; you know that I love you,* even when I don't act like it.

Lord, show me what You want me to do to *Feed Your sheep* and . . .

GOOD MORNING, GOD!
February 29

Galatians 4:4-7

But when the time had fully come, God sent his Son, born of a woman, born under law, to redeem those under law, so that we might receive full rights of sons. Because you are sons, God has sent the Spirit who calls out, "Abba, Father." So you are no longer a slave, but a son; and since you are a son, God has made you also an heir.

Good Morning, God! *Abba Father* is the same as saying "Daddy." What a beautiful thought that I can call the Almighty God of All Creation, Daddy. That is such a term of endearment as the simple faith of a child talking to their father. I am a child of God. I long for such a close relationship I can call You, *Abba Father.* You have brought me into Your family through Your grace and mercy by the sacrifice of Your Son, Jesus Christ. Because of this You have *also made me an heir.* Thank You, Precious Savior.

Lord, help me to realize the privilege it is to be Your heir and show me how to . . .

✠ ✠ ✠

March

GOOD MORNING, GOD!
March 1

1 Peter 5:5b-7

> *. . . All of you, clothe yourselves with humility toward one another, because, "God opposes the proud but shows favor to the humble." Humble yourselves, therefore, under God's mighty hand, that he may lift you up in due time. Cast all your anxiety on him because he cares for you.*

Good Morning, God! Lord, I know my pride is my worst enemy. I think I am in control and everything that is to be done is up to me. I worry and fret about things over which I have no control. How foolish I am. You reign! You are the God of Creation and You set the world into motion. Nothing is done except by Your hand. Help me to humble myself before You and know that You are God.

Let me *cast all my anxiety on You because You care for me* and . . .

GOOD MORNING, GOD!
March 2

Psalm 8:3-5

When I consider your heavens, the work of your fingers, the moon and the stars, which you have set in place, what is mankind that you are mindful of them, human beings that you care for them? You have made them a little lower than the angels and crowned them with glory and honor.

Good Morning, God! Lord, it is true. When I think of Your Majesty and the beauty and wonder of the world You created, I am in awe of the fact that You even consider a sinner such as me. Your scriptures paint a glorious picture of Who You truly are. The God of the universe is my Lord and King. You care for me as a mother loves and protects her children. You love me and have even *made me a little lower than the angels.* Thank You, Lord. My heart overflows with joy in knowing and serving You.

Lord, let me bring You glory in all I do today and . . .

GOOD MORNING, GOD!
March 3

2 Timothy 1:6-9

For the Spirit God gave us does not make us timid, but gives us power, love and self-discipline. So do not be ashamed of the testimony about our Lord or of me his prisoner. Rather, join with me in suffering for the gospel, by the power of God. He has saved us and called us to a holy life – not because of anything we have done but because of his own purpose and grace. This grace was given us in Christ Jesus before the beginning of time.

Good Morning, God! You are a God of grace and mercy. Paul died to himself and became a prisoner in chains to preach Your word. I want to be like that. I want to be brave and proclaim Your Word. Your Spirit *gives us power, love and self-discipline.* You have *saved me and called me to a holy life.* I don't feel as if I have a holy life, but because of Your grace *given in Christ Jesus before the beginning of time,* I am a child of God. I am forgiven and I give You thanks and praise. Thank You, Precious Savior.

Guide my steps today to bring You glory in all I do and . . .

GOOD MORNING, GOD!
March 4

Joshua 1:5-7

No one will be able to stand up against you all the days of your life. As I was with Moses, so I will be with you; I will never leave you nor forsake you. Be strong and courageous, because you will lead these people to inherit the land I swore to their forefathers to give them. Be strong and very courageous to obey all the law my servant Moses gave you; do not turn from it to the right or to the left, that you may be successful wherever you go.

Good Morning, God! You are my rock and my shield. If I follow You and Your direction, *no one will be able to stand up against me all the days of my life.* How awesome is that? I will not *turn from it to the right or to the left.* I will follow wherever You lead. I know that You are with me *all the days of my life* and will guide and protect me. I know the plans You have for me and I want to be successful for You wherever I go.

Lord help me to be strong and courageous for You in order to . . .

GOOD MORNING, GOD!
March 5

Psalm 92:1-4

It is good to praise the Lord and make music to your name, O Most High, to proclaim your love in the morning and your faithfulness at night, to the music of the ten-string lyre and the melody of the harp. For you make me glad by your deeds, O Lord; I sing for joy at the works of your hands.

Good Morning, God! Thank You for this day! Thank You for all Your bounteous blessings! I am so richly blessed I want to shout Your praises. You are my Great and Glorious God. Praise God from Whom all blessings flow. I want to praise You all day long. Don't let me get caught up in the snares of this world and forget how You have blessed me. When everything seems to be going wrong, don't let me forget You are with me and I am Yours. I love You, Lord.

Lord, thank You most of all for . . .

GOOD MORNING, GOD!
March 6

1 John 4:11-13

Dear friends, since God so loved us, we also ought to love one another. No one has ever seen God; but if we love one another, God lives in us and his love is made complete in us. We know that we live in him and he in us, because he has given us of his Spirit.

Good Morning, God! When I think of the great love You have shown me, I am overwhelmed. I feel so unworthy and humbled at the same time. You are a God of love and mercy. You created everyone—great and small, every religion and ethnicity, and You love each of Your children equally. Lord, help me to see everyone as a child of God and not judge by just what I see on the surface. Let me love them as Jesus would love and I will give You all praise and glory.

Lord, help me let Your Spirit reign within me and . . .

GOOD MORNING, GOD!
March 7

Proverbs 17:22

A cheerful heart is good medicine, but a crushed spirit dries up the bones.

Good Morning, God! Lord, in this day and age of so much illness and tragedy, it is really hard to keep a cheerful heart. With our aging society, there are so many who are suffering either from infirmities or calamities. Our families are torn apart and our nation is falling away from You. Lord, let me think of only Your goodness and mercy. Let me remember Your incredible blessings and not dwell on what is falling apart around me. Let me be Your instrument to bring *cheerful hearts* to those who are hurting. We all have so much to be thankful for. Let us dwell on these things and not the bad.

Lord, let my Spirit be filled with Your cheer and . . .

GOOD MORNING, GOD!
March 8

James 2:17-19

In the same way, faith by itself, if it is not accompanied by action, is dead. But someone will say, "You have faith; I have deeds." Show me your faith without deeds, and I will show you my faith by what I do. You believe that there is one God. Good! Even the demons believe that – and shudder.

Good Morning, God! Lord, I know I am not saved by what I do, but I also know that if I love You and serve You it will be reflected in my life. I want to do Your will and work. There are a lot of "good" people in this world who do many "good" things, but unless we have faith and are working for You and Your glory, our *works are dead.* I want to show the world that I love and serve You by all that I do. I want people to know that I serve my God and King in everything I do.

Lord, give me wisdom and discernment to show my faith by . . .

GOOD MORNING, GOD!
March 9

Psalm 16:5-7

Lord, you alone are my portion and my cup; you make my lot secure. The boundary lines have fallen for me in pleasant places; surely I have a delightful inheritance. I will praise the Lord, who consoles me; even at night my heart instructs me.

Good Morning, God! What a joy it is to serve a God of such provision and total security. Just the thought that *I have a delightful inheritance* overwhelms me. This is not of my own doing, but because of Your love for me. There is no way I can earn my salvation. Everything is a gift from You through Your mercy and grace. Lord, don't let me worry about tomorrow. You have already laid it out and I'll walk hand-in-hand with You in complete peace and joy to be Your child.

Thank You, Lord, for Your provision of . . .

GOOD MORNING, GOD!
March 10

Ephesians 1:13-14

And you also were included in Christ when you heard the message of truth, the gospel of your salvation. When you believed, you were marked in him with a seal, the promised Holy Spirit, who is a deposit guaranteeing our inheritance until the redemption of those who are God's possession – to the praise of his glory.

Good Morning, God! When I consider that I am *God's possession,* I am filled with awe and wonder. I feel so unworthy to merit Your love, but Your Spirit lives within me and draws me closer and closer to You. I have *the promised Holy Spirit* through Whom Jesus said we would have the power to do greater things than He. I am so thankful for Your love and sacrifice and the giving of Your Spirit. Lord, I pray I can claim the power I have received. Let me use it to *the praise of Your glory.*

Holy Spirit, pray for me to . . .

GOOD MORNING, GOD!
March 11

Hebrews 12:1-2

Therefore since we are surrounded by such a great cloud of witnesses, let us throw off everything that hinders and the sin that so easily entangles. And let us run with perseverance the race marked out for us, fixing our eyes on Jesus, the pioneer and perfecter of faith. For the joy set before him he endured the cross, scorning its shame, and sat down at the right hand of the throne of God.

Good Morning, God! Lord, when I consider what You have done for me, I am amazed that You love me so much. The term *excruciating* is a derivative of crucifixion. *You endured the cross, scorning its shame.* So many times I find myself taking Your sacrifice for granted and I am so ashamed. You suffered and died for me to be saved. Let me *throw off everything that hinders and the sin that so easily entangles* and devote my life and will to be conformed to Yours.

Lord, let me *run with perseverance the race marked out for me* and . . .

GOOD MORNING, GOD!
March 12

Colossians 3:18-21

Wives, submit yourselves to your husbands, as is fitting in the Lord. Husbands love your wives and do not be harsh with them. Children, obey your parents in everything, for this pleases the Lord. Fathers, do not embitter your children, or they will become discouraged.

Good Morning, God! What a perfect recipe for a perfect family life. In these days when there is so much turmoil and strife in the family, if we would only cling to Your Word and live as you have instructed us, the world would be a much better place. Sometimes it seems that *submitting to your husbands* may not be in vogue. If wives and husbands would submit to each other in love and honor, our lives would be filled with joy and peace. It is when we are selfish and think only of ourselves that we lose sight of Your perfect plan and become *discouraged.*

Lord, help me to submit to You and show me . . .

GOOD MORNING, GOD!
March 13

Psalm 134:1-3

Praise the Lord, all you servants of the Lord who minister by night in the house of the Lord. Lift up your hands in the sanctuary and praise the Lord. May the Lord, the Maker of heaven and earth bless you from Zion.

Good Morning, God! Lord, I love to sing Your praises day and night. I *lift up my hands in the sanctuary and praise the Lord.* Lord, I love to be in Your house and give You all my worship and praise. What a glorious privilege we have that we can gather together and praise You. Lord, I pray for those who live in countries that don't permit their people to worship You. Give them courage and strength to continue to praise Your name. *Maker of heaven and earth bless them from Zion.*

Lord, let me forever sing Your praise and . . .

GOOD MORNING, GOD!
March 14

Isaiah 61:1-2a

The Spirit of the Sovereign Lord is on me, because the Lord has anointed me to proclaim good news to the poor. He has sent me to bind up the brokenhearted, to proclaim freedom for the captives and release from darkness for the prisoners, to proclaim the year of the Lord's favor . . .

Good Morning, God! I love these words of our Lord Jesus Christ for He was truly sent to *proclaim good news to the poor.* I know these words are also for me. You have called me to be Your messenger to proclaim the *Good News* to the world. Give me the words to say, O Lord. Place people in my path who are hungry for Your Word. Use me to show them the way to receive You as their Lord and Savior. Let them see Your Light shining through me *to bind up the brokenhearted, to proclaim freedom for the captives and release from darkness for the prisoners.*

Lord, use me to . . .

GOOD MORNING, GOD!
March 15

Psalm 138:1-3

I will praise you, O Lord, with all my heart; before the gods I will sing your praise. I will bow down toward your holy temple and will praise your name for your love and your faithfulness, for you have exalted above all things your name and your word. When I call, you answered me; you made me bold and stouthearted.

Good Morning, God! *I will praise You, O Lord, with all my heart; before the gods I will sing Your praise.* Lord, I know I put so many gods before You. I am truly sorry. The things of this world are so alluring, but *You have exalted above all things Your name and Your Word.* Help me to hold You above all things. Help me to be *bold and stouthearted.* I know that *when I call, You answer me.* Thank You, my God and King. Thank You for Your *love and faithfulness.*

Lord, keep me from temptation and . . .

GOOD MORNING, GOD!
March 16

Isaiah 38:4-6

Then the word of the Lord came to Isaiah: Go and tell Hezekiah, "This is what the Lord, the God of your father David says: I have heard your prayer and seen your tears; I will add fifteen years to your life. And I will deliver you and this city from the hand of the king of Assyria. I will defend this city."

Good Morning, God! O Lord, when I read scriptures of Your wonder and might, I am in awe. You are a strong God of unimaginable power and yet You are a loving God of tender compassion. You *heard Hezekiah's prayers and saw his tears* and had mercy on him. Who but the Lord God Almighty could add *fifteen years to his life and defend the city from the king of Assyria?* I give You thanks and praise not just because You can, but because You do.

Let me feel Your power and might always and never, never doubt Your love for me. Help me to . . .

GOOD MORNING, GOD!
March 17

Mark 4:38-41

Jesus was in the stern, sleeping on a cushion. The disciples woke him and said to him, "Teacher, don't you care if we drown?" He got up, rebuked the wind and said to the waves, "Quiet! Be still!" Then the wind died down and it was completely calm. He said to his disciples, "Why are you so afraid? Do you still have no faith?" They were terrified and asked each other, "Who is this? Even the wind and the waves obey him!"

Good Morning, God! *"Who is this? Even the wind and the waves obey him!"* Precious Savior, how can I ever have fears and be anxious about the things of this world? You have overcome the world and even nature. You are the Creator and the Conductor of all things. I give my life into Your hands – my heart, my time, my whole being. I want to rest in the security of Your power and love. I love You, Lord.

Keep me so close that . . .

GOOD MORNING, GOD!
March 18

Galatians 1:10-12

Am I now trying to win the approval of human beings, or of God? Or am I trying to please people? If I were still trying to please people, I would not be a servant of Christ. I want you to know, brothers and sisters that the gospel I preached is not of human origin. I did not receive it from any man, nor was I taught it; rather, I received it by revelation from Jesus Christ.

Good Morning, God! Lord, unfortunately I do worry about pleasing others. It is my pride and I am sorry. However, I truly want to please You in everything I do. I pray each morning that everything I do brings You glory. I want to serve You alone. Unfortunately, as the day progresses and I get caught up in the day to day activities, I sometimes find myself trying to please everyone. Help me to see that my first love and priority is You. Let me *be a servant of Christ.*

Show me what I can do for You today, Lord, and . . .

GOOD MORNING, GOD!
March 19

Psalm 98:4-6

Shout for joy to the Lord, all the earth, burst into jubilant song with music; make music to the Lord with the harp, with the harp and the sound of singing, with trumpets and the blast of the ram's horn – shout for joy before the Lord, the King.

Good Morning, God! Lord, when I think of Your goodness and mercy it makes me want to *shout for joy to the Lord.* I am so incredibly blessed and your grace covers me like a silky garment. When I feel Your arms around me, I am swept away into the calm of a beautiful lake – a lake that reflects Your grandeur. I want to dance and sing Your praise all day long. Thank You for all Your blessings. You fill my life with joy.

Lord, let me praise You by . . .

GOOD MORNING, GOD!
March 20

Matthew 4:18-20

Now as Jesus was walking by the Sea of Galilee, He saw two brothers, Simon who was called Peter, and Andrew his brother, casting a net into the sea; for they were fishermen. And He said to them, "Follow Me, and I will make you fishers of men." Immediately they left their nets and followed Him.

Good Morning, God! O Lord, I love the fact that You call ordinary people to be Your disciples. You didn't call the High Priest or the highly educated scholars, but simple people who will *immediately leave their nets and follow You.* Lord, I know You have created each of Your children with a Spiritual Gift to serve You and further Your Kingdom. Let me feel that calling and respond as You would have me to serve where You need me.

Let me be a *fisher of men* and serve You by . . .

GOOD MORNING, GOD!
March 21

Romans 5:8-10

But God demonstrates his own love for us in this: While we were still sinners, Christ died for us. Since we have now been justified by his blood, how much more shall we be saved from God's wrath through him? For if, while we were God's enemies, we were reconciled to him through the death of his Son, how much more, having been reconciled, shall we be saved through his life!

Good Morning, God! How wondrous is Your love, O God. You know my very heart, even better than I know myself, and yet You gave Your Son to die for my sins. It hurts me to think of myself as *God's enemy* and yet, I know when I sin against You it is as if I were Your enemy. I love You, Lord, and am so thankful I can be *reconciled to You through the death of Your Son.* Thank You, Precious Jesus for suffering and dying for me. I love you, Lord.

Lord, guide me today to . . .

GOOD MORNING, GOD!
March 22

Hebrews 1:1-4

In the past God spoke to our ancestors through the prophets at many times and in various ways, but in these last days he has spoken to us by his Son, whom he appointed heir of all things, and through whom also he made the universe. The Son is the radiance of God's glory and the exact representation of his being, sustaining all things by his powerful word. After he had provided purification for sins, he sat down at the right hand of the Majesty in heaven.

Good Morning, God! Loving Father, I love spending time in Your Word to hear the very essence of You speaking directly to me. You sent Your Son who *is the radiance of God's glory and the exact representation of his being,* so that I can truly know You. Help me to see You in Your glory. Let me be so overwhelmed with Your Majesty and fall at Your feet in praise and worship. Let everything I do today bring You glory.

Holy Spirit, pray for me to . . .

GOOD MORNING, GOD!
March 23

Ephesians 5:8-10

For you were once darkness, but now you are light in the Lord. Live as children of light (for the fruit of the light consists in all goodness, righteousness and truth) and find out what pleases the Lord.

Good Morning, God! Lord, I thank You for calling me and working in my life to bring me out of the darkness into the *light in the Lord.* When I consider my former wayward life, I shudder. I thank You for Your prevenient grace that brought me into the Light of Your Presence. When I think of the path of destruction I was walking, I become heartsick. I think of all the time I wasted that I could have been serving You and letting Your Light shine through me to bring others to You. I want to *find out what pleases the Lord* and make that my life's work.

Thank You for Your grace and . . .

GOOD MORNING, GOD!
March 24

Isaiah 44:1-3

But now listen, Jacob, my servant, Israel, whom I have chosen. This is what the Lord says – he who made you, who formed you in the womb, and who will help you: Do not be afraid, Jacob, my servant, Jeshurun [people of Israel], whom I have chosen. For I will pour water on the thirsty land, and streams on the dry ground; I will pour out my Spirit on your offspring, and my blessing on your descendants.

Good Morning, God! So many times in the Scripture You say *do not be afraid.* You know how frail we all are and what a stronghold the great deceiver can have on us. He can tell lies that can cause me to tremble with fear. He can fill me with doubt even as to my worthiness with You. How can I doubt when You tell me that I am *chosen, You will help me and You will pour out You Spirit and blessings.* Thank You for loving me, O Lord. Thank You for Your goodness, grace and mercy for a sinner such as I.

Lord, let me hear what You say and . . .

GOOD MORNING, GOD!
March 25

Matthew 7:1-4

"Do not judge, or you too will be judged. For in the same way you judge others, you will be judged, and with the measure you use, it will be measured to you. Why do you look at the speck of sawdust in your brother's eye and pay no attention to the plank in your own eye? How can you say to your brother, 'Let me take the speck out of your eye, when all the time there is a plank in your own eye?'"

Good Morning, God! Lord, I know why You chose this scripture for me today. I know one of my worse sins is to judge. I pray each day for You to make me stronger and more faithful so that I don't judge and before I know it I'm doing it again. It is so easy to see the sins of others and not myself. Please help me to see my own sins – sins of commission and omission. Help me to be merciful to others as You are merciful to me. Let me see others through the eyes of Christ and I will give You all the glory.

Father, forgive me for being judgmental and . . .

GOOD MORNING, GOD!
March 26

Habakkuk 3:17-19

Though the fig tree does not bud and there are no grapes on the vines, though the olive crop fails and the fields produce no food, though there are no sheep in the pen and no cattle in the stalls, yet I will rejoice in the Lord, I will be joyful in God my Savior. The Sovereign Lord is my strength; he makes my feet like the feet of a deer, he enables me to tread on the heights.

Good Morning, God! Lord, everywhere I look there are troubles in this world. It seems to get worse every day with some new war or disaster, *yet I will rejoice in the Lord, I will be joyful in God my Savior.* Lord, there is no problem greater than You. I can rely on You to get me through the storms of life. You will protect me and hold me close no matter how grim things may seem. *The Sovereign Lord is my strength.* I shall fear no evil because You *make my feet like the feet of a deer, and enable me to tread on the heights.* Praise God.

Lord, let me always look to You for . . .

GOOD MORNING, GOD!
March 27

Zechariah 2:10-11

Shout and be glad, Daughter Zion. For I am coming, and I will live among you, declares the Lord. Many nations will be joined with the Lord in that day and will become my people. I will live among you and you will know that the Lord Almighty has sent me to you.

Good Morning, God! I realize each time I pray The Lord's Prayer and say, *"thy kingdom come,"* I am actually praying for the second coming of the Lord. What a glorious day it will be when all the nations bow down to You and You live among us – when *every knee shall bow and every tongue confess that Jesus Christ is Lord.* Let me be ready and let me share Your message of salvation with everyone I meet so they can be counted within the number of Your saints. I long for *You to live among us.*

Come, Lord Jesus, and . . .

GOOD MORNING, GOD!
March 28

Genesis 3: 8-11

Then the man and his wife heard the sound of the Lord God as he was walking in the garden in the cool of the day, and they hid from the Lord God among the trees of the garden. But the Lord God called to the man, "Where are you?" He answered, "I heard you in the garden, and I was afraid because I was naked; so I hid." And he said, "Who told you that you were naked? Have you eaten from the tree that I commanded you not to eat from?"

Good Morning, God! What a glorious scene this scripture paints of You *walking in the garden in the cool of the day.* This must be what heaven is like – walking with You. What a mess we've made of things because we think we can do it our way. You had the perfect plan for mankind to dwell with You in Paradise and we had to disobey Your command – one simple command. How foolish we are that we think we can hide anything from the Lord God. You know our hearts and desires more than we do ourselves. Forgive me, Lord, for all my sins and prepare me to walk with You in *the garden in the cool of the day* in Eternity.

Lord, help me to keep Your commands by . . .

GOOD MORNING, GOD!
March 29

Galatians 5:22-25

But the fruit of the Spirit is love, joy, peace, forbearance, kindness, goodness, faithfulness, gentleness and self-control. Against such things there is no law. Those who belong to Christ Jesus have crucified the flesh with its passions and desires. Since we live by the Spirit, let us keep in step with the Spirit.

Good Morning, God! Lord, I see that You don't mention the "fruits" of the Spirit but the *fruit* – singular. All these attributes are to be found in each of Your children as a bi-product of being filled with Your Spirit. When we *belong to Christ Jesus we have crucified the flesh with its passions and desires.* You are calling me to keep these attributes in all I do. Help me to *live by the Spirit and keep in step with the Spirit.* Not my will, but Yours alone.

Let this fruit be evident in my life so that . . .

GOOD MORNING, GOD!
March 30

Matthew 6:5-6

"And when you pray, do not be like the hypocrites, for they love to pray standing in the synagogues and on the street corners to be seen by others. Truly I tell you, they have received their reward in full. But when you pray, go into your room, close the door and pray to your Father, who is unseen."

Good Morning, God! Lord, I love to spend my quite time alone with You each morning. I love praying in the morning because I want You to be the source of all I do each day. You are my rock and my shield. I rely on You and Your Word to guide and direct me. I feel Your presence in the quiet, early morning hours when I'm alone with You and before I have to face the world. You give me the courage and wisdom to keep Satan at bay and to be Your servant.

I love You, Lord, and thank You for . . .

GOOD MORNING, GOD!
March 31

Psalm 119:103-106

How sweet are your words to my taste, sweeter than honey to my mouth! I gain understanding from your precepts; therefore I hate every wrong path. Your word is a lamp for my feet, a light on my path. I have taken an oath and confirmed it, that I will follow your righteous laws.

Good Morning, God! O Lord, saturate my body and soul with Your Word. I love spending time in Your Word. I feel so close to You when I'm reading the Bible. I can almost hear Your voice whispering in my ear so that *I gain understanding from Your precepts.* The more I ponder the scriptures, the more I know You and Your goodness and mercy. Your Word is truly *a lamp for my feet and a light on my path* – otherwise, I am in darkness and can't see You.

Lord, light my path today and show me . . .

✠

April

GOOD MORNING, GOD!
April 1

1 Corinthians 9:24-25

Remember that in a race everyone runs, but only one person gets the prize. You also must run in such a way that you will win. All athletes practice strict self-control. They do not win a prize that will fade away but we do it for an eternal prize.

Good Morning, God! Lord, I feel like such a failure. I love You and want to be Your servant, but I feel I never give You my very best. I am too caught up in my own desires and in the glitter of the world. I run, but I don't give it all I have. I need to discipline myself to be the best I can be for You and Your Kingdom. You created me to be the best. I just need to turn my life and will over to You. Answer my prayer, O Lord, and help me to be strong for You.

Thank You, Lord, for I know You hear my prayer and will help me to . . .

GOOD MORNING, GOD!
April 2

Psalm 37:1-4

Do not fret because of evil men or be envious of those who do wrong; for like the grass they will soon wither, like green plants they will soon die away. Trust in the Lord and do good; dwell in the land and enjoy safe pasture. Delight yourself in the Lord and he will give you the desires of your heart.

Good Morning, God! Why is it that it seems so many times the people who do wrong prosper beyond those who try to do what is right? There is no joy in ill-gotten gain – there may be monetary profit, but there is also anguish and fear that goes along with it. I do trust You, Lord and I try my very best to do what is good. I have a clear conscience and I have Your peace. I do *delight myself in You and You do give me the desires of my heart.* I am completely blessed.

Lord, the desire of my heart is to serve You and . . .

GOOD MORNING, GOD!
April 3

2 Chronicles 20:12, 15

O our God, will you not judge them? For we have no power to face this vast army that is attacking us. We do not know what to do, but our eyes are upon you. He said: "Listen, King Jehoshaphat and all who live in Judah and Jerusalem! This is what the Lord says to you: 'Do not be afraid or discouraged because of this vast army. For the battle is not yours, but God's.'"

Good Morning, God! *God, once again You tell me "Do not be afraid or discouraged."* You are with me no matter what *vast army is attaching me.* It is so encouraging to know that the *battle is not mine, but God's.* Praise God! I can go through this day knowing that I have nothing to fear. It is not what I do but what You do through me that matters. I don't have to carry the weight of the world on my shoulders. You will win every battle for me.

Thank You, Lord, for being with me and getting me through . . .

GOOD MORNING, GOD!
April 4

John 15:11-14

I have told you this so that my joy may be in you and that your joy may be complete. My command is this: Love each other as I have loved you. Greater love has no one than this, that he lay down his life for his friends. You are my friends if you do what I command.

Good Morning, God! *The greatest of these is love.* There is no greater love than the love You have for me, Precious Savior. You suffered and died for me and now You call me *friend.* My *joy is complete* because it is Your joy! There is no other joy than the Joy of the Lord. All the material things of this world may offer happiness temporarily but Your joy is forever. I am filled with joy because I am Your child. Thank You, Lord.

Lord, teach me to love as You love and . . .

GOOD MORNING, GOD!
April 5

Joshua 6:2-5

Then the Lord said to Joshua, "See, I have delivered Jericho into your hands, along with its king and its fighting men. Do this for six days. Have seven priests carry trumpets of rams' horns in front of the ark. On the seventh day, march around the city seven times, with the priests blowing the trumpets. When you hear them sound a long blast on the trumpets, have all the people give a loud shout; then the wall of the city will collapse and the people will go up, every man straight in."

Good Morning, God! You tell me that *Your ways are not my ways.* This doesn't sound like a very good battle plan and yet it is perfect, because it is Your plan. Help me to always remember that all I have to do is what You ask, even when it doesn't appear to be the plan I would make, and You will provide the victory.

Lord, thank You for *delivering Jericho into my hands* and help me to . . .

GOOD MORNING, GOD!
April 6

Romans 1:16-17

I am not ashamed of the gospel, because it is the power of God for the salvation of everyone who believes: first for the Jew, then for the Gentile. For in the gospel righteousness from God is revealed, a righteousness that is by faith from first to last, just as it is written: "The righteous will live by faith."

Good Morning, God! I love spending time in Your Word for it shows me the *power of God for the salvation of everyone who believes.* You reveal everything to me through the Bible, and I am not ashamed to proclaim every word. I do believe every Word is God-breathed. My faith comes from reading and hearing Your Words. *For in the gospel righteousness from God is revealed* and *"The righteous will live by faith."*

Lord, give me the righteousness of faith to . . .

GOOD MORNING, GOD!
April 7

1 John 2:15-17

Do not love the world or anything in the world. If anyone loves the world, the love of the Father is not in him. For everything in the world – the cravings of sinful man, the lust of his eyes and the boasting of what he has and does -- comes not from the Father but from the world. The world and its desires pass away, but the man who does the will of God lives forever.

Good Morning, God! Lord, it is so hard not to get caught up in the *cravings of sinful man, the lust of his eyes and the boasting of what he had and does.* I know these things are from the lies of Satan and not from You. I find myself trying to impress people and "keep up". Forgive me, Lord. I know this is wrong. Help me to understand that these material things are not Your plan. The only thing I need is You and my salvation and I am rich beyond the world's fondest dreams.

Let me *store up my treasures in heaven* and . . .

GOOD MORNING, GOD!
April 8

Colossians 1:9-10

For this reason, since the day we heard about you, we have not stopped praying for you and asking God to fill you with the knowledge of his will through all spiritual wisdom and understanding. And we pray this in order that you may live a life worthy of the Lord and may please him in every way; bearing fruit in every good work, growing in the knowledge of God,

Good Morning, God! O Lord, I long to *be filled with the knowledge of Your will through spiritual wisdom and understanding.* I want to give my life to You and serve You and praise You every day. I *want to please You in every way.* I want to *grow in knowledge* each day and know You better and love You more. I surrender my life to You and Your love   for me. Lord, let me *please you in every way.*

Lord, let me *bear fruit in every good work* and . . .

GOOD MORNING, GOD!
April 9

Revelation 1:17-18

When I saw him, I fell at his feet as though dead. Then he placed his right hand on me and said: "Do not be afraid. I am the First and the Last. I am the Living One; I was dead, and behold I am alive for ever and ever! And I hold the keys of death and Hades."

Good Morning, God! Once again You tell me, *"Do not be afraid."* Lord, I am amazed when John was taken to heaven to write the Revelation and he saw You in all Your Glory he *fell at Your feet as though dead.* John spent three years with You in Your earthly ministry and yet, when he saw Your Glory, he was overcome. He had spent time with You as a man and now You are God, seated at the right hand of the Father. I'm sure I will also be overcome when I see You face-to-face. Praise God! You are an awesome God!

Lord, show me Your Glory and help me to . . .

GOOD MORNING, GOD!
April 10

Psalm 51:1-5

Have mercy on me, O God, according to your unfailing love; according to your great compassion blot out my transgressions. Wash away all my iniquity and cleanse me from my sin. For I know my transgressions, and my sin is always before me. Against you, you only, have I sinned and done what is evil in your sight, so that you are proved right when you speak and justified when you judge.

Good Morning, God! Lord, You know how I have failed You and sinned against You. Forgive me, I pray. Please *wash away all my iniquity and cleanse me from my sin. Against You and You only, have I sinned and done what is evil in Your sight.* I am so thankful that because I have been washed by the Blood of Jesus Christ I no longer have to carry the weight of my sin around every day. I am forgiven! Thank You, Sweet Jesus, *according to Your great compassion.*

Lord, help me to forgive as You forgive and . . .

GOOD MORNING, GOD!
April 11

Malachi 3:8b-10

"But you ask, 'How do we rob you?' "In tithes and offerings. You are under a curse – the whole nation of you – because you are robbing me. Bring the whole tithe into the storehouse, that there may be food in my house. Test me in this," says the Lord Almighty, "and see if I will not throw open the floodgates of heaven and pour out so much blessing that you will not have room enough for it."

Good Morning, God! Lord, this is the only place in the Bible that You say, *"Test me in this."* I know it is true because I have heard Your call to tithe and realize that all I have is given by Your Hand. You have truly *thrown open the floodgates of heaven and poured out so much blessing that there is not room for it.* I am truly blessed. I will acknowledge You and *bring the whole tithe into the storehouse.*

Thank, You, Lord for Your blessings and . . .

GOOD MORNING, GOD!
April 12

Romans 10:15-17

And how can they preach unless they are sent? As it is written, "How beautiful are the feet of those who bring good news!" But not all the Israelites accepted the good news. For Isaiah says, "Lord, who has believed our message?" Consequently, faith comes from hearing the message, and the message is heard through the word of Christ.

Good Morning, God! I know that *faith comes from hearing the message.* We have to know Your Word to receive the gift of Your *faith.* Send me forth to be Your messenger of *good news.* Let Your message flow through me continually and let people have faith because of Your Word proclaimed through me by Your Spirit. I know that alone, I can do nothing, but with You *all things are possible. Here I am, Lord. Send me.*

Lord use me to further Your Kingdom by . . .

GOOD MORNING, GOD!
April 13

Psalm 25:7-10

Remember not the sin of my youth and my rebellious ways; according to your love remember me, for you are good, O Lord. Good and upright is the Lord; therefore he instructs sinners in his ways. He guides the humble in what is right and teaches them his way. All the ways of the Lord are loving and faithful for those who keep the demands of his covenant.

Good Morning, God! O God, please *remember not the sin of my youth.* I am so sad when I think of all the years I wasted in the wilderness. I was a Christian but I was not in a relationship with You and serving You. I am so thankful You have led me in Your ways. I humble myself before You and ask for Your direction in my life. Help me stay on Your path for *all the ways of the Lord are loving and faithful for those who keep the demands of his covenant.*

Lord, *guide me in what is right* so that . . .

GOOD MORNING, GOD!
April 14

1 Kings 8:22-24

Then Solomon stood before the altar of the Lord in front of the whole assembly of Israel, spread out his hands toward heaven and said: "Lord, the God of Israel, there is no God like you in heaven above or on earth below -- you who keep your covenant of love with your servants who continue wholeheartedly in your way. You have kept your promise to your servant David my father; with your mouth you have promised and with your hand you have fulfilled it – as it is today."

Good Morning, God! Lord, the Bible is filled with Your promises. Why do I ever doubt them? *There is no God like you in heaven above or on earth below.* You will always keep Your promises. There is no way that You can't keep them for You are God – *with your mouth you have promised and with your hand you have fulfilled it. There is no God like You in heaven above or on earth below.* Praise be to You, O God!

Lord, let Your promises be in my heart today and . . .

GOOD MORNING, GOD!
April 15

John 5:24-25

"Very truly I tell you, whoever hears my word and believes him who sent me has eternal life and will not be judged but has crossed over from death to life. Very truly I tell you, a time is coming and has now come when the dead will hear the voice of the Son of God and those who hear will live."

Good Morning, God! What comforting words – *whoever hears my word and believes him who sent me has eternal life and will not be judged but has crossed over from death to life.* Lord, I do believe with all my heart. I love to study Your Word and feed on every sentence, but I have skimmed over the part where *I will not be judged.* Praise God! I am cleansed by the Blood of Jesus Christ. I will stand before You as white as snow. Thank You, Sweet Jesus.

Lord, let me live for You and . . .

GOOD MORNING, GOD!
April 16

1 Thessalonians 1:4-5

We know that God loves you, dear brothers and sisters, and that he chose you to be his own people. For when we brought you the Good News, it was not only with words but also with power, for the Holy Spirit gave you full assurance that what we said was true. And you know that the way we lived among you was further proof of the truth of our message.

Good Morning, God! What blessed *assurance* to know that God loves me. Who am I that the God of Creation would know me and love me? *You have chosen me to be Your own.* Thank You for giving me the *Good News* and the gift of *The Holy Spirit, not only with words but also with power.* Your Holy Spirit opens my eyes and heart to know You and understand Your Word. Let me use that power to bring others to know You as well.

Let my life reflect Your Spirit and . . .

GOOD MORNING, GOD!
April 17

Luke 24:46-47

Yes, it was written long ago that the Messiah must suffer and die and rise again from the dead on the third day. With my authority, take this message of repentance to all the nations beginning in Jerusalem: "There is forgiveness of sins for all who turn to me."

Good Morning, God! Precious Savior, when I consider how You suffered and died for me it breaks my heart. You are the One perfect Son of God. You are all goodness, grace and love and yet You had to die in such a terrible way for my sins. I give You all praise and glory and honor, Lord. It was my sins that nailed You to the cross. I do earnestly repent and beg Your forgiveness. *With Your authority, I will take this message of repentance to all the nations.*

I do turn to You, Lord. Please forgive me for . . .

GOOD MORNING, GOD!
April 18

1 Kings 19:12-13

After the earthquake there was a fire, but the Lord was not in the fire. And after the fire there was the sound of a gentle whisper. Then Elijah heard it, he wrapped his face in his cloak and went out and stood at the entrance of the cave. And a voice said, "What are you doing here, Elijah?"

Good Morning, God! So many times I expect You to be present in the great things. You are so majestic and powerful I expect to hear thunder and see lightning in Your presence. I look for You in the astonishing occurrences. Teach me to be still and listen for the *sound of a gentle whisper.* Let me hear Your voice. Oh for a Word from You, O Lord. I long to be so close I can hear Your whisper.

Hold me close today, Lord, and . . .

GOOD MORNING, GOD!
April 19

Judges 6:14-16

The Lord turned to him and said, "Go in the strength you have and save Israel out of Midian's hand. Am I not sending you?" "But Lord," Gideon asked, "how can I save Israel? My clan is the weakest in Manasseh, and I am the least of my family." The Lord answered, "I will be with you, and you will strike down all the Midianites together."

Good Morning, God! Lord, I feel so weak and powerless. I feel lost and confused. I know You have called us all to be Your disciples, but how can You use me? I can do nothing on my own, but when You are with me, I can do all things. It isn't about what I can do, but what You can do through me. I trust You to give me the strength I need to accomplish Your will. I know You *will be with me and we will strike down all the Midianites together.* Thank You, Lord, for calling me and using me to do Your work.

I have no limitations with You. Help me to . . .

GOOD MORNING, GOD!
April 20

Psalm 122:6-9

Pray for the peace of Jerusalem: "May those who love you be secure. May there be peace within your walls and security within your citadels." For the sake of my brothers and friends, I will say, "Peace be with you." For the sake of the house of the Lord our God, I will seek your prosperity.

Good Morning, God! With all the unrest in Israel at this time, I pray for peace for Your people. You say there will always be war, but I earnestly pray for peace. I know You say You will bless those who bless Israel. Let the world rally behind Your Chosen People and bring them Your peace *for the sake of my brothers and friends.* Let them be secure and prosperous. *May there be peace within their walls and security within their citadels.* Let them find complete peace with You.

Lord, show me what I can do to help bring this peace and . . .

GOOD MORNING, GOD!
April 21

Genesis 21:5-7

Abraham was a hundred years old when his son Isaac was born to him. Sarah said, "God has brought me laughter, and everyone who hears about this will laugh with me." And she added, "Who would have said to Abraham that Sarah would nurse children? Yet I have borne him a son in his old age."

Good Morning, God! The story of the birth of Isaac is the quintessential example of faith and trust in You. Abraham and Sarah waited years and years for a son – even past the age of child-bearing and yet You always keep Your promises. So many times I think that things have to be logical and in the order of nature, but not with You. Sarah and Abraham tried to "help You out" by having a son with Hagar. We know what a disaster that became. Let me know that You are in control and it isn't up to me to fix things. Give me the faith to completely trust You for everything in my life. I know Your Word is true.

Thank You for the laughter in my life and . . .

GOOD MORNING, GOD!
April 22

Ephesians 4:15-16

We will hold to the truth in love, becoming more and more in every way like Christ, who is the head of his body, the church. Under his direction, the whole body is fitted together perfectly. As each part does its own special work, it helps the other parts grow, so that the whole body is healthy and growing and full of love.

Good Morning, God! Lord, what a beautiful plan You have orchestrated. The church is the *body of Christ*. We are united to grow the church and love one another. *Under his direction, the whole body is fitted together perfectly.* You have created a *special work* for me *to help the other parts grow.* I am blessed to be part of the body and pray You will guide and direct me as to what I am to do *so that the whole body is healthy and growing and full of love.*

Here I am, Lord, send me out to . . .

GOOD MORNING, GOD!
April 23

Matthew 14:28-30

"Lord, if it's you," Peter replied, "tell me to come to you on the water." "All right, come," Jesus said. So Peter went over the side of the boat and walked on the water toward Jesus. But when he looked around at the high waves, he was terrified and began to sink. "Save me, Lord!" he shouted.

Good Morning, God! I love when You say, *"All right, come."* You are always asking me to come to You and walk with You in all of life's situations. As long as I keep my eyes on You I am safe and can *walk on water.* When I take my eyes off You and look at the *high waves around me, I am terrified and begin to sink.* When I think I can do things in my own strength, I fail. But, all I have to do is call out to You and You will save me. Thank You, Lord.

Lord, I need You today to . . .

GOOD MORNING, GOD!
April 24

Colossians 2:13-15

When you were dead in your sins and in the uncircumcision of your sinful nature, God made you alive with Christ. He forgave us all our sins, having canceled the written code, with its regulation, that was against us and they stood opposed to us; he took it away, nailing it to the cross. And having disarmed the powers and authorities, he made a public spectacle of them, triumphing over them by the cross.

Good Morning, God! What glorious Good News! *You have made me alive with Christ.* The old person is dead and You have created a new life in me. You have taken away my sin. You *took it away, nailing it to the cross.* You are a mighty and awesome Savior. I can rest in the truth that my sins are forgiven because of Your great sacrifice on the cross. Because of Your love, I no longer carry the burden, but You take it from me. I am surrounded by Your peace.

Thank You, Lord, for . . .

GOOD MORNING, GOD!
April 25

1 Corinthians 3:9-11

For we are God's fellow workers; you are God's field, God's building. By the grace God has given me, I laid a foundation as an expert builder, and someone else is building on it. But each one should be careful how he builds. For no one can lay any foundation other than the one already laid, which is Jesus Christ.

Good Morning, God! Lord, *I am Your fellow worker.* You *have laid a foundation as an expert builder* and perfect foundation for Your church – *Jesus Christ.* I love to hear that I am *God's field, God's building.* You are using me to grow Your church and further the Kingdom. On Christ alone I stand – the rock solid foundation of my faith. I will not waiver or fall for You are leading me.

Thank You Lord for the strong foundation of my faith and help me to . . .

GOOD MORNING, GOD!
April 26

John 15:1-4

"I am the true vine, and my Father is the gardener. He cuts off every branch in me that bears no fruit, while every branch that does bear fruit, he prunes so that it will be even more fruitful. You are already clean because of the word I have spoken to you. Remain in me, and I will remain in you. No branch can bear fruit by itself; it must remain in the vine. Neither can you bear fruit unless you remain in me.

Good Morning, God! Lord, I have experienced Your pruning away *every branch in me that bears no fruit.* Pruning, or cutting away, is very painful, but I know that it is necessary to produce the *fruit* that You desire in me. Thank You for loving me enough to take the time to prune me. Thank You for delivering me from my sin and creating a new life in me. Let me *remain in the vine* and *bear the fruit* of Your righteousness.

Lord, *remain in me* and . . .

GOOD MORNING, GOD!
April 27

James 1:5-6

If any of you lacks wisdom, he should ask God, who gives generously to all without finding fault, and it will be given to him. But when he asks, he must believe and not doubt, because he who doubts is like a wave of the sea, blown and tossed by the wind. That man should not think he will receive anything from the Lord; he is a double-minded man, unstable in all he does.

Good Morning, God! I am so thankful that when *I ask for wisdom You give generously to all without finding fault, and it will be given to him.* I truly desire wisdom to determine Your will for my life. Give me the faith to not doubt Your Word. I know Your promises are true. You will give me wisdom and I will do Your will. Thank You, Lord, for Your love and mercy.

Show me Your will for . . .

GOOD MORNING, GOD!
April 28

John 1:3-5

Through him [Jesus] all things were made; without him nothing was made that has been made. In him was life, and that life was the light of all mankind. The light shines in the darkness and the darkness has not overcome it.

Good Morning, God! Lord, when I am in my darkest hour and feel there will be no end to my sorrow, You appear with Your Radiant Light. Your light enables me to see things through Your eyes. It enables me to see all the beauty and majesty around me; things You created to delight all Your children. It lets me see You more clearly. It lights my path to follow You in the ways of Your righteousness. Thank You, Lord.

Lord, let Your light shine through me and . . .

GOOD MORNING, GOD!
April 29

John 17:3-5

Now this is eternal life: that they know you, the only true God, and Jesus Christ, whom you have sent. I have brought you glory on earth by finishing the work you gave me to do. And now, Father, glorify me in your presence with the glory I had with you before the world began.

Good Morning, God! Precious Jesus, You gave up everything for me. You left the splendors of heaven and came to die on a cross for me that I may have eternal life. You have shown me who God the Father is with His love and compassion. Lord, help me *finish the work you gave me to do.* I want to *bring You glory* by living a life worthy of Your grace and mercy. I long to see You in Your glory in heaven.

Thank You, Jesus for . . .

GOOD MORNING, GOD!
April 30

Galatians 3:3-5

Are you so foolish? After beginning by means of the Spirit, are you now trying to finish by means of the flesh? Have you experienced so much in vain – if it really was in vain? So again I ask does God give you his Spirit and work miracles among you by the works of the law or by your believing what you heard?

Good Morning, God! Oh, Lord, this scripture describes me to a tee. I start out with the best intentions and even pray for your guidance and direction, then I decide that I need to help You. *Am I so foolish?* Lord, give me the grace to let Your Spirit *work your miracles among me* and let me follow You alone. Let me realize that with man things are impossible but with You all things are possible.

Lord, I believe. Help me to follow You and . . .

May

GOOD MORNING, GOD!
May 1

Ezra 8:21-23

There, by the Ahava Canal, I proclaimed a fast so that we might humble ourselves before our God and ask him for a safe journey for us and our children, with all our possessions. . . "The gracious hand of our God is on everyone who looks to him, but his great anger is against all who forsake him." So we fasted and petitioned our God about this, and he answered our prayer.

Good Morning, God! Lord, why do I always think prayer is my last resort. "I" don't know what to do so all I can do is pray. Prayer should be first in everything I do. *So we fasted and petitioned our God about this, and he answered our prayer.* Lord, give me wisdom to call upon You in every situation. I know You will answer my prayers. *The gracious hand of our God is on everyone who looks to Him.* Help me to *look* to You first and not rely on myself.

Thank you for answering my prayers and . . .

GOOD MORNING, GOD!
May 2

2 Chronicles 20:17-18

You will not have to fight this battle. Take up your positions; stand firm and see the deliverance the Lord will give you, Judah and Jerusalem. Do not be afraid; do not be discouraged. Go out to face them tomorrow, and the Lord will be with you. Jehoshaphat bowed down with his face to the ground and all the people of Judah and Jerusalem fell down in worship before the Lord.

Good Morning, God! Lord, so many times You tell me not to worry, *do not be afraid; do not be discouraged* and *You will be with me.* Why is this so hard for me to accept? I know You and Love You, Lord; I believe You and have faith in You. Let me just rejoice in the fact that when I *go out and face them tomorrow, the Lord will be with me.* I know this is true and I give You thanks and praise for being my God.

Jesus, help me to see and feel You beside me in every battle and . . .

GOOD MORNING, GOD!
May 3

Hebrews 12:4-6

In your struggle against sin, you have not yet resisted to the point of shedding your blood. And have you completely forgotten this word of encouragement that addresses you as a father addresses his son? It says, "My son, do not make light of the Lord's discipline, and do not lose heart when he rebukes you, because the Lord disciplines the one he loves, and he chastens everyone he accepts as his son."

Good Morning, God! Lord, I am so thankful to be addressed as Your child. I do *struggle against sin* but have not come even close to *shedding my blood.* I pray daily and ask for Your forgiveness and gladly receive Your discipline *because the Lord disciplines the one he loves, and he chastens everyone he accepts as his son.* Let me receive Your discipline with joy because it is a gift from You, my Father. Praise God from Whom all blessings flow.

Lord, teach me to . . .

GOOD MORNING, GOD!
May 4

Matthew 5:43-45

"You have heard that it was said, 'Love your neighbor and hate your enemy.' But I tell you, love your enemies and pray for those who persecute you, that you may be children of your Father in heaven. He causes his sun to rise on the evil and the good, and sends rain on the righteous and unrighteous. . ."

Good Morning, God! Lord, I pray You give me Your Spirit of love and forgiveness *to love my enemies and pray for them*. It is especially hard *to pray for those who persecute me*, but I do so because You tell me to. As I pray I feel Your presence and the sad circumstance of those for whom I'm praying becomes so evident. I do actually pity them and pray for Your mercy on them.

Lord, let me claim Your love and mercy today by . . .

GOOD MORNING, GOD!
May 5

John 1:11-13

He came to that which was his own, but his own did not receive him. Yet to all who did receive him, to those who believed in his name, he gave the right to become children of God – children born not of natural descent, nor of human decisions or a husband's will, but born of God.

Good Morning, God! Lord, it is so sad when people don't receive You. You have come to be the Lord and Savior of all. You have freely given Your blood to wash away all sin. I am eternally blessed to be *born of God*. I am a *child of God* and an heir to Your Kingdom. What a glorious thought. Fill me with Your Words and Spirit so that I can proclaim Your Good News to all and let them know they can also have the wonderful inheritance for those who are a *child of God*.

Lord, give me the courage to . . .

GOOD MORNING, GOD!
May 6

2 Timothy 1:6-7

For this reason I remind you to fan into flame the gift of God, which is in you through the laying on of my hands. For God did not give us a spirit of timidity, but a spirit of power, of love and of self-discipline.

Good Morning, God! Lord, let me realize the power I have from Your Spirit. I know that You are with me and will give me the courage to go forth in Your Name. Let me not be timid about sharing the gospel. Give me the words to move mountains for You. Let me show Your love to everyone so they can know You and love You and enjoy the everlasting joy of being Your child.

Lord, help me to *fan into flame the gift* You have given me to . . .

GOOD MORNING, GOD!
May 7

John 15:15-17

My prayer is not that you take them out of the world but that you protect them from the evil one. They are not of the world, even as I am not of it. Sanctify them by the truth; your word is truth.

Good Morning, God! What a glorious thought that Jesus is praying for me. He is praying *that I not be taken out of this world but that I would be protected from the evil one.* You have called me to proclaim Your Word and Satan is doing all he can to stop me, but he has lost all his power. Lord, I claim this promise and know that You will strengthen me against the evils of this world. *I am not of this world for* I am Your child. *Sanctify me by the truth; Your word is truth.* My home is in heaven and not here on earth, but it is my joy to serve You until You call me home.

Thank You, Lord, for praying for me and help me to . . .

GOOD MORNING, GOD!
May 8

2 Peter 1:19-21

And we have the word of the prophets made more certain, and you will do well to pay attention to it, as to a light shining in a dark place, until the day dawns and the morning star rises in your hearts. Above all, you must understand that no prophecy of Scripture came about by the prophet's own interpretation. For prophecy never had its origin in the will of man, but men spoke from God as they were carried along by the Holy Spirit.

Good Morning, God! Lord, I love spending time alone with You in Your Word for I know this is how You speak directly to me. Your Word *is as to a light shining in a dark place.* In my quiet time, I hear Your voice and I am filled with awe. The God of the universe is communing with me and I with Him. Let me take every Word into my heart and use it for Your glory. *Carry me along by the Holy Spirit.* Praise God!

Lord, fill me with Your Word and send me forth to . . .

GOOD MORNING, GOD!
May 9

Psalm 106:1-3

Praise the Lord. Give thanks to the Lord, for he is good; his love endures forever. Who can proclaim the mighty acts of the Lord or fully declare his praise? Blessed are those who act justly, who always do what is right.

Good Morning, God! Lord, I will praise you all day long. You *are good and Your love endures forever.* I have so much to be thankful for. *Who can proclaim the mighty acts of the Lord or fully declare his praise?* I am filled with awe and wonder at all Your blessings for which I am not worthy. But, You continually shower me with blessing upon blessings. I will praise You in all I say and do. I shout Your praise from every ounce of my being.

Thank You, Lord, for all Your blessings and . . .

GOOD MORNING, GOD!
May 10

1 Corinthians 6:19-20

Do you now know that your body is a temple of the Holy Spirit, who is in you, whom you have received from God? You are not your own; you were bought at a price. Therefore honor God with your body.

Good Morning, God! Lord, I am so ashamed when I think of all the trash I put into my body every day. I fill myself with the garbage of this world. I get caught up in all kinds of things I know are not pleasing to You. Not only in the food I consume, but the things I allow into my mind. Help me to have a clean Spirit, O God. Help me to dwell only on You and what is good.

Lord, let Your Holy Spirit work in me to . . .

GOOD MORNING, GOD!
May 11

1 Samuel 18:1, 3-4

After David had finished talking with Saul, Jonathan became one in spirit with David, and he loved him as himself. And Jonathan made a covenant with David because he loved him as himself. Jonathan took off the robe he was wearing and gave it to David, along with his tunic, and even his sword, his bow and his belt.

Good Morning, God! Lord, we are so blessed with the relationships You place in our lives. My friends and family lift me up and hold me accountable. I am surrounded by Christian brothers and sisters whom I love and who love me. We are not meant to be alone in this world. Your gift of family and friendship is very special and proclaims Your deep love for me. Thank You, Lord.

Lord, help me to be a friend to others by . . .

GOOD MORNING, GOD!
May 12

Jeremiah 18:5-6

Then the word of the Lord came to me: "O house of Israel, can I not do with you as this potter does?" declares the Lord. "Like clay in the hands of the potter, so are you in my hand."

Good Morning, God! O Lord, I surrender to You. My life is in Your mighty hands. Mold me and make me what You want for me. Shape me into the servant You desire me to be. I love to feel You working in my life. I know You are creating a new person who will be more Christ-like and stronger to do Your will. Make me more loving and compassionate toward others. Use me, Lord, and send me forth to declare the glory of the Lord.

Lord, let me be like clay in Your hands so that. . .

GOOD MORNING, GOD!
May 13

Romans 1:5-7

Through him and for his name's sake, we received grace and apostleship to call people from among all the Gentiles to the obedience that comes from faith. And you also are among those who are called to belong to Jesus Christ. To all in Rome who are loved by God and called to be saints: Grace and peace to you from God our Father and from the Lord Jesus Christ.

Good Morning, God! Lord, I am engulfed in Your sea of grace and peace. As hard as I try, I am continually doing things I know aren't right. I pray and ask for Your help to stop sinning, but I fall short. Give me *the obedience that comes from faith.* It is by the grace of Your forgiveness that I can face each day. I am surrounded by Your peace even when I know I am a sinner. The blood of Jesus Christ has cleansed me white as snow. Thank You, Jesus.

Lord, thank You for loving me so much that You . . .

GOOD MORNING, GOD!
May 14

2 Samuel 12:5-7a

David burned with anger against the man and said to Nathan, "As surely as the Lord lives, the man who did this deserves to die! He must pay for that lamb four times over, because he did such a thing and had no pity." Then Nathan said to David, "You are the man!"

Good Morning, God! How easy it is for me to see the sins of others and set myself above them in my own eyes. Yet, if I would look into my heart and see all the hidden sins, I would be crushed with remorse because *I did such a thing and had no pity.* Lord, help me to see the sins I tuck away and never bring to light. Help me to recognize them and repent and ask for Your forgiveness. Thank You for Your grace to me a sinner.

Lord, I am sorry for . . .

GOOD MORNING, GOD!
May 15

Psalm 86:1-5

Hear, O Lord, and answer me, for I am poor and needy. Guard my life, for I am devoted to you. You are my God; save your servant who trusts in you. Have mercy on me, O Lord, bring joy to your servant for to you, O Lord, I lift up my soul. You are forgiving and good, O Lord, abounding in love to all who call to you.

Good Morning, God! I call on You each day for forgiveness and mercy for *I am devoted to you.* Keep me close to You so that I am continually in Your presence and feel Your mercy. Let me not go as the world goes, but keep me from sinning *for to You, O Lord, I lift up my soul.* I am Yours. Take my life and mold me into the perfect plans You have for me. Let me be Your servant, Lord.

You are forgiving and good, O Lord. Forgive me for . . .

GOOD MORNING, GOD!
May 16

2 Chronicles 32:6-8a

He appointed military officers over the people and assembled them before him in the square at the city gate and encouraged them with these words: "Be strong and courageous. Do not be afraid or discouraged because of the king of Assyria and the vast army with him, for there is a greater power with us than with him. With him is only the arm of flesh, but with us is the Lord our God to help us and to fight our battles."

Good Morning, God! Lord, I face battles each day. Satan is continually shooting his flaming arrows all around me. *I will be strong and courageous.* I will not be discouraged because these battles seem insurmountable *for there is greater power with me than with him.* You are with me and *the Lord our God will help me to fight my battles.* Praise God.

Lord, when I am faced with battles help me to . . .

GOOD MORNING, GOD!
May 17

Revelation 21:23, 26-27

The city does not need the sun or the moon to shine on it, for the glory of God gives it light, and the Lamb is its lamp. The glory and honor of the nations will be brought into it. Nothing impure will ever enter it, nor will anyone who does what is shameful or deceitful, but only those whose names are written in the Lamb's book of life.

Good Morning, God! Oh, Lord, how beautiful. *The city does not need the sun or the moon to shine on it, for the glory of God gives it light, and the Lamb is its lamp.* You are truly the Light of the world. What a wonderful plan You have for Your people. I can't wait to be standing in that Light and worshiping You always. I am thankful I know my name is written *in the Lamb's book of life.* I am forgiven because You died for my sins and I have asked for Your mercy. Thank You, Jesus.

Come, Lord Jesus, come and . . .

GOOD MORNING, GOD!
May 18

Mark 5:35-36

While Jesus was still speaking, some men came from the house of Jairus, the synagogue ruler. "Your daughter is dead," they said. "Why bother the teacher anymore?" Ignoring what they said, Jesus told the synagogue ruler, "don't be afraid; just believe."

Good Morning, God! Lord, even when things seem completely out of control and calamity abounds, You are there. Even when things seem utterly hopeless and the news is the worst, You are still the King. I love when You say, *"don't be afraid; just believe."* I do believe and my faith and trust are in You alone. You are my Redeemer King. Praise God!

Lord, increase my faith to . . .

GOOD MORNING, GOD!
May 19

Luke 17:15-19

One of them, when he saw he was healed, came back, praising God in a loud voice. He threw himself at Jesus' feet and thanked him — and he was a Samaritan. Jesus asked, "Were not all ten cleansed? Where are the other nine? Was no one found to return and give praise to God except this foreigner?" Then he said to him, "rise and go; your faith has made you well."

Good Morning, God! Lord, how many times do You offer me Your healing grace and I *do not return and give praise to God?* It is so easy to take Your mercy and goodness for granted. I hate myself when I do that. Help me to be ever thankful and singing Your praises, for You are good. Thank You for a *faith that has made me well* in the midst of all the ills of this world.

Lord, I *praise You in a loud voice* and . . .

GOOD MORNING, GOD!
May 20

Genesis 3:1-4

Now the serpent was more crafty than any of the wild animals the Lord God had made. He said to the woman, "Did God really say, 'You must not eat from any tree in the garden?'" The woman said to the serpent "we may eat fruit from the trees in the garden, but God did say, 'You must not eat fruit from the tree that is in the middle of the garden and you must not touch it, or you will die.'" "You will not surely die," the serpent said to the woman.

Good Morning, God! The enemy is truly *more crafty than any of the wild animals* and he uses every deceitful trick he can contrive to make me believe his lies. He is the great deceiver and the "father of all lies." Don't let me get caught up in his traps. Don't let me believe his lies when he tries to convince me that I am unworthy of Your love. Help me to see through his schemes and trust only in You.

Lord, give me wisdom to . . .

GOOD MORNING, GOD!
May 21

Luke 7:20, 22

When the men came to Jesus, they said, "John the Baptist sent us to you to ask, 'Are you the one who was to come, or should we expect someone else?'". . .So he replied to the messengers, "Go back and report to John what you have seen and heard: The blind receive sight, the lame walk, those who have leprosy are cured, the deaf hear, the dead are raised, and the good news is preached to the poor."

Good Morning, God! Lord, I see Your mighty works all around me and yet at times my faith can falter. How can this be when I know I am a child of the Most High God! My Savior lives, and Your Spirit lives within me. Increase my faith that I may never waiver or fall away. Let me proclaim Your mighty works to all that they may believe.

Lord, open my eyes that . . .

GOOD MORNING, GOD!
May 22

Nehemiah 9:30-31

For many years you were patient with them. By your Spirit you admonished them through your prophets. Yet they paid no attention, so you handed them over to the neighboring peoples. But in your great mercy you did not put an end to them or abandon them, for you are a gracious and merciful God.

Good Morning, God! Lord, I am so thankful You are patient with me. You have given me Your Word and Your Spirit to lead me in the paths of righteousness. You have not *abandoned me.* Forgive me that in so many instances I have *paid no attention.* Thank You for being a *gracious and merciful God.* Lead me in the way that You would have me go. Show me the way to be more like Jesus.

Lord, teach me to be patient and merciful to . . .

GOOD MORNING, GOD!
May 23

Jeremiah 1:4, 7-8

The word of the Lord came to me, saying, "Before I formed you in the womb I knew you, before you were born I set you apart; I appointed you as a prophet to the nations." . . . But the Lord said to me, "Do not say, 'I am only a child.' You must go to everyone I send you to and say whatever I command you. Do not be afraid of them, for I am with you and will rescue you," declares the Lord.

Good Morning, God! Lord, if this isn't the perfect scripture for the pro-life movement, there is none. *Before I formed you in the womb I knew you.* We are each formed by You, O Lord and You knew us before we are born. All life is sacred to You. Send me forth in Your Name, O Lord, to proclaim Your message of Life and Salvation for all. *I will not be afraid for You will rescue me.*

Lord, thank You for creating me and *setting me apart* to . . .

GOOD MORNING, GOD!
May 24

Genesis 3:20-23

Adam named his wife Eve, because she would become the mother of all the living. The Lord God made garments of skin for Adam and his wife and clothed them. And the Lord God said, "The man has now become like one of us, knowing good and evil. He must not be allowed to reach out his hand and take also from the tree of life and eat and live forever." So God banished him from the Garden of Eden to work the ground from which he had been taken.

Good Morning, God! What a loving God You are. When Adam and Eve sinned and were hiding because they were naked, You *made garments of skin for Adam and his wife and clothed them.* They knew what they did was wrong but You had compassion on them. You could have just been mad at them and banished them from the Garden, but that is not Your nature. You don't want to see Your children hurting even when it is caused by their own sinfulness.

Lord, thank You for loving me so much and help me to . . .

GOOD MORNING, GOD!
May 25

Matthew 6:7-8

And when you pray, do not keep on babbling like pagans, for they think they will be heard because of their many words. Do not be like them, for Your Father knows what you need before you ask him.

Good Morning, God! Lord, I know there is great power in prayer. You tell us to *pray without ceasing.* You don't mean that I have to close myself away and remain on my knees all day. You want me to pray to You as I'm talking to my Father. You don't need flowery words or long prayers. You simply want to commune with me. I don't pray to change Your mind, but to know You and Your will for me. *You know what I need before I ask.* Prayer is simply a means of spending time in Your presence and growing in my relationship with You.

Thank You, Lord, for hearing my prayers and . . .

GOOD MORNING, GOD!
May 26

Hebrews 7:25-26

Therefore he is able to save completely those who come to God through him, because he always lives to intercede for them. Such a high priest meets our need — one who is holy, blameless, pure, set apart from sinners, exalted above the heavens.

Good Morning, God! Precious Jesus, You are so good to me *because You live to intercede for me.* Lord, when I think of You praying for me, I cannot imagine that You, the Lord of all Creation, would be mindful of me. I am so insignificant in the scheme of Your realm and yet You intercede for me. This is love that is beyond my comprehension. This is Your love. The Love of Christ for His people. I am so blessed. Thank You, Lord.

Lord, let me intercede for others as You do for me so that . . .

GOOD MORNING, GOD!
May 27

Joshua 1:8-9

Do not let this Book of the Law depart from your mouth; meditate on it day and night, so that you may be careful to do everything written in it. Then you will be prosperous and successful. Have I not commanded you? Be strong and courageous. Do not be terrified; do not be discouraged, for the Lord your God will be with you wherever you go.

Good Morning, God! Lord, I need to spend more time in Your Word. I have the best intentions each day but inevitably something comes up and steals my time away. Please forgive me. I want to know Your Word and keep it close to my heart. I want to be *strong and courageous* for You. Give me the faith and words to shout the Good News to everyone I meet. I want everyone to know You and all the goodness and mercy You shower on Your children.

Lord, let me *not be terrified*, but strong to . . .

GOOD MORNING, GOD!
May 28

Isaiah 41:13-14

"For I am the Lord, your God, who takes hold of your right hand and says to you, Do not fear; I will help you. Do not be afraid . . .for I myself will help you, declares the Lord, your Redeemer, the Holy One of Israel."

Good Morning, God! O God, what loving words from a Father to His rebellious child. Your love is unconditional. No matter how badly I stray, You will *take hold of my right hand* and lead me to be the person You want me to be. You tell me, *Do not be afraid for I myself will help you.* This is comforting beyond words, Father God. I know I am loved by the *Lord, my Redeemer, the Holy One of Israel.* Thank you for loving me, the sinner that I am.

Give me the faith to place my life in Your hands so that . . .

GOOD MORNING, GOD!
May 29

Acts 2:38-39

Peter replied, "Repent and be baptized, every one of you, in the name of Jesus Christ for the forgiveness of your sins. And you will receive the gift of the Holy Spirit. The promise is for you and your children, and for all who are far off – for all whom the Lord our God will call."

Good Morning, God! Lord, what a beautiful promise. I do *repent in the name of Jesus Christ for the forgiveness of my sins.* I am filled with *the gift of the Holy Spirit.* What a glorious gift You have given *Your children.* Your Spirit lives within me and I have the power to do all things through You. Guide and direct me to fulfill this promise to Your glory. Thank You for *calling me* to serve You, Lord.

Lord, help me to show Your glory by . . .

GOOD MORNING, GOD!
May 30

Jeremiah 33:2-3

"*This is what the Lord says, he who made the earth, the Lord who formed it and established it – the Lord is his name: Call to me and I will answer you and tell you great and unsearchable things you do not know.*"

Good Morning, God! Lord, I spend so much time praying and wondering what Your will is for my life. I need to stop trying to find all understanding through my own knowledge and wisdom. I need to turn to You and You will give me the answers *and tell me great and unsearchable things.* You are all knowledge and wisdom. You tell us in the book of James, that *you draw near to those who draw near to You.* I will pray and depend on You to give me the wisdom I need.

Lord, show me the *unsearchable things* so I can share them with . . .

GOOD MORNING, GOD!
May 31

Psalm 35:17-19a

The righteous cry out, and the Lord hears them; he delivers them from all their troubles. The Lord is close to the brokenhearted and saves those who are crushed in spirit. A righteous man may have many troubles, but the Lord delivers him from them all; . . .

Good Morning, God! You are an amazing, loving, caring God. When I cry out, You hear me. You are so close to me and You alone know when I am *brokenhearted and crushed in spirit.* You comfort me and hold me through every storm in my life. Whether a spring rain or a raging hurricane, You are there with me. I can go through this day knowing that whatever troubles may befall me, my Lord and Savior will deliver me *from them all.*

Lord, deliver me today from . . .

✤ ✤ ✤

June

GOOD MORNING, GOD!
June 1

Numbers 7:24-26

The Lord bless you and keep you; the Lord make his face shine upon you and be gracious to you; the Lord turn his face toward you and give you peace.

Good Morning, God! What a glorious way to start the day covered in Your blessings. You are the God of rich blessings. You shower me with Your love and mercy. You call me to be Your child. You are my Father. How wondrous is it that You love me. I can conquer anything the evil one throws at me because I am filled with Your peace. Thank you, Father God. Thank You!

I will walk in Your love today and . . .

GOOD MORNING, GOD!
June 2

1 Timothy 6:9-10

People who want to get rich fall into temptation and a trap and into many foolish and harmful desires that plunge men into ruin and destruction. For the love of money is a root of all kinds of evil. Some people, eager for money, have wandered from the faith and pierced themselves with many griefs.

Good Morning, God! Don't let me get caught in the trap of striving to please the world and have all the world's false treasures. These are the things that destroy men's souls. Let me lay up my treasure in heaven. Let me follow You all the days of my life and know that You are my all in all. You alone are God and You alone are worthy to be praised. Let me enjoy the benefits of being Your child and know that is far more valuable than all the world has to offer.

Deliver me from the love of things that keep me from You and help me to . . .

GOOD MORNING, GOD!
June 3

Acts 15:10-11

Now then, why do you try to test God by putting on the necks of the disciples a yoke that neither we nor our fathers have been able to bear? No! We believe it is through the grace of our Lord Jesus that we are saved, just as they are.

Good Morning, God! Lord, we are all the same in Your eyes. We are Your children whom You created and love. Give me the grace not to be prejudiced against anyone. Show me how to love as You love for it is by Your grace *that we are saved*. I should love everyone with the Love of Christ. Don't let Satan distort my vision. Let me see through Your eyes.

Lord, with Your grace I will . . .

GOOD MORNING, GOD!
June 4

Zephaniah 3:16-17

On that day they will say to Jerusalem, "Do not fear, O Zion; do not let your hands hang limp. The Lord your God is with you, he is mighty to save. He will take great delight in you, he will quiet you with his love, he will rejoice over you with singing."

Good Morning, God! I can't imagine how much You love me. You *are with me and mighty to save.* Is it possible that You delight in me? Is it possible that You will *rejoice over me with singing?* I am so incredibly blessed by You, O Lord. Put me to work for You. Show me what You would have me do. I want to serve You. I know I can't merit Your love, but that is why You are God. God is love!

All praise and glory to You O Lord. Let me show my praise by . . .

GOOD MORNING, GOD!
June 5

1 Chronicles 29:10-11

David praised the Lord in the presence of the whole assembly, saying, "Praise be to you, O Lord, God of our father Israel, from everlasting to everlasting. Yours, O Lord, is the greatness and the power and the glory and the majesty and the splendor, for everything in heaven and earth is yours. . ."

Good Morning, God! No wonder David was a *man after Your own heart.* Oh that I could express such praises to You. David truly knew You and all Your glory. I pray that I can feel this praise deep down in my soul. I pray that my prayers are pleasing to You and can invoke Your Spirit within me to praise You with every breath I take.

Lord, I give You all my praise for . . .

GOOD MORNING, GOD!
June 6

Zechariah 1:2-3

The Lord was very angry with your forefathers. Therefore tell the people: This is what the Lord Almighty says: 'Return to me, declares the Lord Almighty, and I will return to you,' says the Lord Almighty.

Good Morning, God! You are truly *the Lord Almighty.* I try to live my life under my own authority. I think I know what I am doing and I think it is my responsibility to fix my life. Lord, help me to see that it is You alone who is in control and I have to give all authority to You. Bless me to be a blessing. Help me to totally surrender everything to you.

Return to me so that I . . .

GOOD MORNING, GOD!
June 7

Proverbs 4: 5-7

Get wisdom, get understanding; do not forget my words or swerve from them. Do not forsake wisdom, and she will protect you; love her, and she will watch over you. Wisdom is supreme; therefore get wisdom. Though it cost all you have, get understanding.

Good Morning, God! The wisdom of the Lord is more precious than anything in this world. To know You and love You is the greatest gift You give us. I want to know You more and more every day. I want my life to be saturated with Your Word and with knowledge of You. I want to understand how deep is Your love and how much You want me to be covered in Your grace. Thank You, Lord.

Give me the wisdom to . . .

GOOD MORNING, GOD!
June 8

Philippians 3:7-9a

But whatever was to my profit I now consider loss for the sake of Christ. What is more, I consider everything a loss compared to the surpassing greatness of knowing Christ Jesus my Lord, for whose sake I have lost all things. I consider them rubbish that I may gain Christ and be found in him, not having a righteousness of my own. . .

Good Morning, God! O Lord, all I want is to *be found in You.* I want my whole life to be a monument to Your glory. Nothing brings me more joy than to be in Your Word and to witness Your greatness. The things that used to be so important to me are no longer of any value. The only true meaning in my life is to proclaim You to the world. All I have is in You, my Lord and my Redeemer.

Lord, fill me with Your righteousness so that I may . . .

GOOD MORNING, GOD!
June 9

Proverbs 2:6-8

For the Lord gives wisdom, and from his mouth come knowledge and understanding. He holds victory in store for the upright, he is a shield to those whose walk is blameless, for he guards the course of the just and protects the way of his faithful ones.

Good Morning, God! Dear Lord, I pray for wisdom. I want to know Your will and hear Your voice. I know that when I spend time in Your Word and in prayer, Your Spirit is working in me to bring me closer to You and to Your will for my life. I need Your wisdom to receive Your guidance to stay on the path to righteousness.

Help me to seek You in everything today and show me the way to . . .

GOOD MORNING, GOD!
June 10

Matthew 5:6

Blessed are those who hunger and thirst for righteousness, for they will be filled.

Good Morning, God! Your Beatitudes are among the most precious words You gave to us. You give us Your guidance for a life filled with Your grace and love. Lord, I do truly *hunger and thirst* to know You and to live a life worthy of Your righteousness. The only hope I have of being *filled* is through You and Your Holy Spirit. Everything else is dross. Bless me to be a blessing, Lord. Use me to further Your Kingdom and bring people closer to you. Let them see Your Light in me.

Lord, I want to be filled with You in order to share Your . . .

GOOD MORNING, GOD!
June 11

Psalm 27:13-14

I am still confident of this: I will see the goodness of the Lord in the land of the living. Wait for the Lord; be strong and take heart and wait for the Lord.

Good Morning, God! I am confident that You promise *goodness and mercy shall follow me all the days of my life.* I need to stop and let You be God! I need to let You be in control. I need to *wait* for You to make me *strong.* I need to seek Your guidance and trust You to lead me. Why do I think I have to fix everything myself? Let me *see the goodness of the Lord.* Let me place my life in Your hands and wait for the glorious things You have planned for me.

Dear God, today please let me . . .

GOOD MORNING, GOD!
June 12

Matthew 13:18-19

"Listen then to what the parable of the sower means: When anyone hears the message about the kingdom and does not understand it, the evil one comes and snatches away what was sown in his heart. This is the seed sown along the path."

Good Morning, God! Open my heart so that when I read Your Word Your Spirit can interpret it for me and I will understand. Let Your Word fill my very being and let me know You better. Show me Your goodness and grace. Help me to also realize that Satan is constantly lurking around trying to pull me away from You. He is the father of all lies. Let Your Word so permeate my heart that he can't deceive me.

Holy Spirit, pray for me to . . .

GOOD MORNING, GOD!
June 13

Matthew 12:36-37

But I tell you that men will have to give account on the day of judgment for every careless word they have spoken. For by your words you will be acquitted, and by your words you will be condemned.

Good Morning, God! This scripture scares me to death. I can restrain many of my actions but I know I am so bad about the things I say. I can commit murder with my tongue and sometimes it isn't carelessly but maliciously. Help me to bridle my tongue and use only words that build people up and not tear them down. Let my words be the Words of Christ. Let them be a beautiful symphony to those who hear and let them know Your love for us all.

Help me to glorify You today by . . .

GOOD MORNING, GOD!
June 14

Jeremiah 29:12-14a

Then you will call upon Me and come and pray to Me, and I will listen to you. You will seek Me and find Me when you seek Me with all your heart. I will be found by you and bring you back from captivity.

Good Morning, God! Sometimes I feel so far away from You. I don't know how it happens but it is a terrible feeling. It is caused by the hidden sin in my life. It is as if I am trying to hide from You as Adam and Eve did in the Garden. I know that You have not moved, so it has to be me. Lord, prepare my mind to truly pray and seek You with my whole heart. Thank You for Your promise that You will listen and I'll find You and be close again.

I love being close to You and . . .

GOOD MORNING, GOD!
June 15

Acts 20: 22-24

"And now, compelled by the Spirit, I am going to Jerusalem, not knowing what will happen to me there. I only know that in every city the Holy Spirit warns me that prison and hardships are facing me. However, I consider my life worth nothing to me, if only I may finish the race and complete the task the Lord Jesus has given me – the task of testifying to the gospel of God's grace."

Good Morning, God! I realize how insignificant I am in the order of Your creation, but I also realize that You have given me a very important task. You have called each of us to testify to the gospel of Your grace. Lord, I want to shout it from the rooftops. Your grace is an unmerited gift – something I could never deserve or purchase, but You lavish it upon all your children. Let me be aware of the price You paid for my grace. Let me be ever thankful and not take it for granted. Let me run the race with all that is within me. Let me never stop until you call me home and I'll give you all the glory.

Help me to . . .

GOOD MORNING, GOD!
June 16

John 14:19-21

Before long, the world will not see me anymore, but you will see me. Because I live, you also will live. On that day you will realize that I am in my Father, and you are in me, and I am in you. Whoever has my commands and obeys them, he is the one who loves me. He who loves me will be loved by my Father, and I too will love him and show myself to him.

Good Morning, God! Your promises are so beautiful, Lord. You, the Lord of Creation, live within me. Who am I to receive such blessings? I do love You, Lord, but I'm not always obedient. I hate myself for making my will more important than Yours. I let Satan harden my heart to the point that I don't even realize I am being disobedient. Help me to stand firm against Satan. Let me put on the full armor of God to fend off his fiery arrows.

Lord, show Yourself to me. I want to see you. I want to feel Your arms around me so that I can . . .

GOOD MORNING, GOD!
June 17

Luke 10:40-42

But Martha was distracted by all the preparations that had to be made. She came to him and asked, "Lord, don't you care that my sister has left me to do the work by myself? Tell her to help me!" "Martha, Martha," the Lord answered, "You are worried and upset about many things, but only one thing is needed. Mary has chosen what is better and it will not be taken away from her."

Good Morning, God! Sweet Jesus, how I long to sit at Your feet and listen to all You have to tell me. Let me be focused on listening to Your voice. Unfortunately, I live in the world and get tangled in its spider webs of rushing and worrying. I am strangled by the "stuff" I have to do and sometimes I don't even have time to pray.

Lord, let me realize I'm never too busy to pray. I need You in my life and I need to commune with you daily. It is the softest part of my day. I love to be in Your presence.

Let me choose what is better so . . .

GOOD MORNING, GOD!
June 18

1 Samuel 14:6

Jonathan said to his young armor-bearer, "Come, let's go over to the outpost of those uncircumcised fellows. Perhaps the Lord will act in our behalf. Nothing can hinder the Lord from saving, whether by many or by few."

Good Morning, God! Lord, I have seen Your saving mercies. I have witnessed Your miracles. While I admire Jonathan's faith, I ask you to strengthen mine. My faith should be as strong as his or Paul's or John's. Why do I falter, Lord? You always act on our behalf. You can drown Pharaoh's armies with the crashing down of the Red Sea or bring flood rains from a cloud the size of a man's fist. You are Almighty God!

Lord, please act on my behalf and strengthen my faith to . . .

GOOD MORNING, GOD!
June 19

Exodus 33:12-13

Moses said to the Lord, "You have been telling me, 'Lead these people,' but you have not let me know whom you will send with me." You have said, "I know you by name and you have found favor with me. If you are pleased with me, teach me your ways so I may know you and continue to find favor with you. Remember that this nation is your people."

Good Morning, God! Lord, I don't see how there is very much in me that could be pleasing to you and that I should find Your favor. I struggle every minute of every day to please You but I continually fall short. Actually, fall short is too mild an expression. I fail miserably.

So, I pray, Lord, that since I find favor in Your sight, *teach me your ways.* Let me be more like Christ. Let His light shine through me. Let others see You through me. I want to *continue in Your favor.*

I am so thankful that . . .

GOOD MORNING, GOD!
June 20

1 Peter 2:9-10

But you are a chosen people, a royal priesthood, a holy nation, a people belonging to God, that you may declare the praises of Him who called you out of darkness into His wonderful light. Once you were not a people, but now you are the people of God; once you had not received mercy, but now you have received mercy.

Good Morning, God! *I belong to you, God.* I have been chosen by You to proclaim the Good News to all the world. How can I be a *royal priesthood*? I can because I have Your Spirit dwelling within me giving me the words to say and directing my actions to be worthy of You. You have entrusted me to declare Your praises. I no longer live in darkness but in Your *wonderful light* – the light that guides my path closer and closer to You. Lord, I *have received Your mercy* and I am a new creation.

Use me, Lord, to . . .

GOOD MORNING, GOD!
June 21

1 Thessalonians 5:15-18

Make sure that nobody pays back wrong for wrong, but always try to be kind to each other and to everyone else. Be joyful always; pray continually; give thanks in all circumstances, for this is God's will for you in Christ Jesus.

Good Morning, God! Father God, how amazing is it that Your will for me is to be joyful always? I am truly joyful because I have the Joy of the Lord. I am joyful because I know that my Redeemer lives. I am joyful because I know that I will spend eternity with You. My joy is not derived from circumstances in this world no matter how great they may be. My joy is in knowing that I am a child of God and I am loved beyond anything I can understand.

For all this, I give You thanks and . . .

GOOD MORNING, GOD!
June 22

Nahum 1:7

The Lord is good, a refuge in times of trouble. He cares for those who trust in Him.

Good Morning, God! Oh, God, how comforting it is to know that You are always there *in times of trouble.* It seems that troubles can surround me and choke me, depriving me of the strength I need to go on. I do trust in You, Lord, and I know that no matter what I am facing, You will lead me through it to build my faith and hope in You. *You are an ever present help in trouble.* Whom shall I fear?

I love to dwell in the refuge of Your arms and feel Your presence. I want to lie beside you as John did and feel You right next to me. I want to . . .

GOOD MORNING, GOD!
June 23

Psalm 66: 1-4

Shout with joy to God, all the earth! Sing the glory of His name; make His praise glorious! Say to God, "How awesome are Your deeds! So great is your power that your enemies cringe before you. All the earth bows down to you; they sing praise to you, they sing praise to your name."

Good Morning, God! Oh, God, I do *shout for joy* and *sing praises to the glory of Your Name.* You are such an awesome God. *How awesome are Your deeds!* You are constantly by my side showering me with your blessings of love and grace and mercy. I want the whole world to know You and the joy it is to be Your child. Help me to know you better and love you more.

Let Your Spirit set me on fire for You and help me to . . .

GOOD MORNING, GOD!
June 24

2 Corinthians 12:8-10

Three times I pleaded with the Lord to take it away from me. But he said to me, "My grace is sufficient for you, for my power is made perfect in weakness." Therefore I will boast all the more gladly about my weaknesses, so that Christ's power may rest on me. That is why, for Christ's sake, I delight in weaknesses, in insults, in hardships, in persecutions, in difficulties. For when I am weak, then I am strong.

Good Morning, God! Oh, Lord, My God, I am such a weak person. I know You and love You, but it seems I fail continually to keep Your Word. Lord, let me be aware of Your Power that is in me. You have given me Your Spirit to make me strong in my weakness. Let me turn to You for all my cares and needs. Let me delight in my weakness and let your Power rest on me and bring me Your strength and joy.

Father, today I want to . . .

GOOD MORNING, GOD!
June 25

2 Corinthians 5:10

"For we must all appear before the judgment seat of Christ, that each one may receive what is due him for the things done while in the body, whether good or bad."

Good Morning, God! Oh, Lord, I have the entire day ahead of me to choose to do good or evil. You know I love you and I strive to do Your will but, inevitably, I fall short. I get so caught up in the world that I don't keep You in the forefront.

Help me, Lord. Let me feel Your constant presence. Let me feel Your gentle hand in the small of my back guiding me. Let me feel Your Spirit burning inside me. Let me be so on fire for You that others can see Your Light through me.

I ask this in the name of Jesus Christ. All praise, honor and glory to you, My King. And, Lord, today I especially need . . .

GOOD MORNING, GOD!
June 26

Ephesians 2:8-10

For it is by grace you have been saved, through faith—and this is not from yourselves, it is the gift of God— not by works, so that no one can boast. For we are God's handiwork, created in Christ Jesus to do good works, which God prepared in advance for us to do.

Good Morning, God! Father God, when I think of how deep Your love is for me, I am amazed. I, like, Paul, am one of the world's greatest sinners, yet You love me anyway. Your Grace is truly amazing. I know that I am your child and heir to your glorious Kingdom. What an assurance this is. What joy fills my heart! I am a child of God!

Lord, let me take Your grace into the world today. Let me show grace and mercy to everyone I encounter and I will give You all the glory. Father, help me today to . . .

GOOD MORNING, GOD!
June 27

Daniel 10: 10-11

A hand touched me and set me trembling on my hands and knees. He said, "Daniel, you who are highly esteemed, consider carefully the words I am about to speak to you, and stand up, for I have now been sent to you." And when he said this to me, I stood up trembling.

Good Morning, God! Oh, God, as I read these words I tremble. I can feel the power in them – Your Power, and I am in awe. Lord, there is so much I don't understand, but I hunger and thirst for Your Word. I love to be in Your Word and see how mighty You are. For it is in Your Word that I come to know You as my close, loving Father and Friend.

Every minute with You fills my heart with Your joy and I want . . .

GOOD MORNING, GOD!
June 28

Isaiah 43: 1

> *But now, this is what the LORD says—*
> *he who created you, Jacob,*
> *he who formed you, Israel:*
> *"Do not fear, for I have redeemed you;*
> *I have summoned you by name; you are mine.*

Good Morning, God! Our great God and Creator, how can it be that You know my name? You are so completely filled with grace and mercy. Help me at all times to know this. In the midst of my trials and troubles let me lean upon You. You know my name! You love me and protect me. Not that I am worthy, but because *You have redeemed me and I am Yours.*

You have called me by name, Lord, and I want to . . .

GOOD MORNING, GOD!
June 29

Psalm 84:10-11

> *Better is one day in your courts than thousands elsewhere; I would rather be a doorkeeper in the house of my God than dwell in the tents of the wicked.*
>
> *For the Lord God is a sun and shield; the Lord bestows favor and honor; no good thing does he withhold from those whose walk is blameless.*

Good Morning, God! Lord, I am so thankful that I am in Your courts. I spent so much of my life on the outside and in the wilderness. But, You wooed me and called me back to You – back home to Your courts. Thank you, Lord. I deeply regret all the time I wasted in the *tents of the wicked.*

You are *my sun and shield*. You are the true light of the world. If we walk in Your light, we will stay on the straight path.

Lord Jesus, help me to walk blamelessly. Help me to . . .

GOOD MORNING, GOD!
June 30

John 13:34-35

"A new command I give you: Love one another. As I have loved you, so you must love one another. By this all men will know that you are my disciples, if you love one another."

Good Morning, God! Precious Savior, You **are** love. You loved me before I was born. You loved me when I was far away from you. You love me, the sinner that I am. I am so thankful for all Your goodness, grace and mercy. Because of Your great love for me, in order to honor You, I truly love Your children. Lord, I love them because we are all Your children, heirs to Your Kingdom.

It is my joy to call them brothers and sisters in Christ. I want everyone to know You. I want to be numbered with your disciples. Lord, with Your help I want to . . .

July

GOOD MORNING, GOD!
July 1

1 Peter 1:3-5

Praise be to the God and Father of our Lord Jesus Christ! In His great mercy he has given us new birth into a living hope through the resurrection of Jesus Christ from the dead, and into an inheritance that can never perish, spoil or fade. This inheritance is kept in heaven for you, who through faith are shielded by God's power until the coming of the salvation that is ready to be revealed in the last time.

Good Morning, God! Precious Father, your mercy endures forever. You love us and have freely given us Your Son for our salvation and have forgiven all our sins. You have removed them as far as the east is from the west. My heart is bursting with Your love and grace. Lord, let me constantly be aware of Your gifts and to grow in faith and fellowship with You. Thank You for the hope and rich inheritance I receive as Your child.

Lord, increase my faith so that I might . . .

GOOD MORNING, GOD!
July 2

1 Samuel 16:7

But the Lord said to Samuel, "Do not consider his appearance or his height, for I have rejected him. The Lord does not look at the things man looks at. Man looks at the outward appearance but the Lord looks at the heart."

Good Morning, God! Precious Savior, it is You who has all authority on heaven and earth. You show love and mercy to all. You comfort, strengthen and guide me each day. You fill me with Your joy and peace. How desolate my existence would be without You.

In light of Your love, who am I to judge anyone? How can I think it is my job when I know it is Yours? Help me to see others through Your eyes so that I may . . .

GOOD MORNING, GOD!
July 3

John 15:7-8

If you remain in Me and My words remain in you, ask whatever you wish, and it will be given to you. This is to My Father's glory that you bear much fruit, showing yourselves to be My disciples.

Good Morning, God! Lord, I want to remain in You and feel Your presence in everything today. Help me to grow in Your Word. I want to live for You alone and share Your Good News with everyone. I want them to be filled with the peace that only You can give. Let Your Spirit guide me to Your will not mine.

Lord, if it is Your will . . .

GOOD MORNING, GOD!
July 4

2 Chronicles 7:14-15

If my people, who are called by my name, will humble themselves and pray and seek My face and turn from their wicked ways, then will I hear from heaven and will forgive their sin and will heal their land.

Good Morning, God! Oh, God, we have strayed so far off the path of Your righteousness. This great "Nation Under God" has become a den of immorality, unfaithfulness, greed and evil. We love the laws of man above the Laws of our God. All we are concerned with is our pleasure and want it NOW! *Let us humble ourselves and pray and seek Your face and turn from our wicked ways.* Forgive us we pray.

Show us how to come back to you and . . .

GOOD MORNING, GOD!
July 5

Joshua 3:5

Joshua told the people, "Consecrate yourselves for tomorrow the Lord will do amazing things among you."

Good Morning, God! You are amazing, God. You show Yourself to us daily in all Your glory and majesty. You love us so much You made the world in beautiful color. You could have made it in black-and-white and we would never have known the difference.

I can't wait to see what You have in store for my life today. Cleanse me of my sins so that I can be close to You. Show me Your will and I will dedicate myself to You.

Show me Your glory and . . .

GOOD MORNING, GOD!
July 6

Isaiah 6:8

Then I heard the voice of the Lord saying, "Whom shall I send? And who will go for us?" And I said, "Here am I. Send me!"

Good Morning, God! Lord, my favorite hymn is *Blessed Assurance.* I love the lyrics: *serving my Savior all the day long.* I know You have called each of us to be Your servants according to the Spiritual Gifts You have given us. I love serving You and being the hands and feet of Christ in a broken world.

My greatest joy is to be Your servant. You have blessed me incredibly and I want to share that blessing with others.

Lord, grant that I may . . .

GOOD MORNING, GOD!
July 7

Luke 5:15-16

Yet the news about Him spread all the more, so that crowds of people came to hear Him and to be healed of their sickness. But Jesus often withdrew to lonely places and prayed.

Good Morning, God! Precious Lord, I love my quiet time with You each morning before I plunge head-long into the chaotic world outside. Spending time alone with You fills me with Your Word for me this day. I am strengthened and empowered with Your Spirit within me. What a glorious way to start each day.

I am encouraged that Your Precious Son spent time alone with you. If He needed to pray then how much more do I?

Lord, I pray . . .

GOOD MORNING, GOD!
July 8

Mark 9:22b-24

"But if you can do anything, take pity on us and help us." "If you can?" said Jesus. "Everything is possible for him who believes." Immediately the boy's father exclaimed, "I do believe; help me overcome my unbelief!"

Good Morning, God! Oh, God, I know that You are faithful and true and nothing is impossible for you, but so many times I find myself thinking as the boy's father, *I do believe; help me overcome my unbelief!* Sometimes when I am in the midst of tribulation I forget how powerful You are. You parted the Red Sea, provided manna and quail for the Israelites in the wilderness and raised Your Son from the dead. How can I ever doubt You? Help me today to remember that *Everything is possible for him who believes.*

Because I know Your promises are true . . .

GOOD MORNING, GOD!
July 9

Romans 8:26-27

In the same way, the Spirit helps us in our weakness. We do not know what we ought to pray for, but the Spirit Himself interceded for us with groans that words cannot express. And he who searches our hearts knows the mind of the Spirit, because the Spirit intercedes for God's people in accordance with the will of God.

Good Morning, God! Lord, You know me better than I know myself. There are so many times that I really don't know exactly for what I should be praying, but You know. When I consider that the Holy Spirit is praying for me *in groans that words cannot express*, I am overwhelmed. I know the power of prayer but I can't imagine the power of the prayer of the Holy Spirit. Who am I that You should pray for me?

Because I love You, Lord, I give You thanks and praise for your love and mercy to me and I want to . . .

GOOD MORNING, GOD!
July 10

Acts 2:45-47

Selling their possessions and goods, they gave to anyone as he had need. Every day they continued to meet together in the temple courts. They broke bread in their homes and ate together with glad and sincere hearts, praising God and enjoying the favor of all the people.

Good Morning, God! Father God, I wish it could be like this today. I get so caught up in the world and the selfish desires of my own heart that I don't stop to realize that praising You and serving others is the greatest joy there can be in this world. You tell us the greatest commandment is to love You and to love one another. Help me to put You first in all I do and think today. Show me where I can serve others and bring them Your joy.

Let today be about You and not . . .

GOOD MORNING, GOD!
July 11

1 Peter 5:8-9

Be self-controlled and alert. Your enemy the devil prowls around like a roaring lion looking for someone to devour. Resist him, standing firm in the faith, because you know that your brothers throughout the world are undergoing the same kind of suffering.

Good Morning, God! Oh God, how complacent we become just trip-tropping through life thinking we are in control and all is well. There is nothing Satan loves more! He is aware of our complacency and is ready to devour us at any moment. He is very shrewd and will creep in one inch at a time until he has us.

Satan is the father of all lies and convinces us that in our trials You have forgotten us. Why should You care for a sinner like me? Lord, I know I need to stand firm and not listen to these lies that distort my faith. I know You are my loving, faithful Father and Satan is an evil liar.

Thank you for . . .

GOOD MORNING, GOD!
July 12

Micah 6:8

He has showed you, O man, what is good. And what does the Lord require of you? To act justly and to love mercy and to walk humbly with your God.

Good Morning, God! What do you require of me Lord? This doesn't sound like a huge request compared to the blessings and wonders we receive every day. I pray that I can be the person you want me to be. I pray for Your wisdom to be just and merciful. I pray for Your Spirit to make me humble before You. I know You hate pride. Help me to bow before You in complete submission. I can't think of any better circumstance than to be humbly before You.

Show me what is good so that I . . .

GOOD MORNING, GOD!
July 13

Daniel 10:12

Then he continued, "Do not be afraid, Daniel. Since the first day that you set your mind to gain understanding and to humble yourself before your God, your words were heard, and I have come in response to them."

Good Morning, God! Lord, it is so comforting to know that You hear my prayers and they are answered. *Since the first day that* I began to pray, You have heard every word. You know what my requests are before I utter them. You *have come in response to them.* Help me to keep You close throughout this day. Let me feel Your Power coursing through my very being. Put me to work for You, Precious Savior.

Knowing You are right by my side I . . .

GOOD MORNING, GOD!
July 14

Psalm 84:11-12

For the Lord God is a sun and shield; the Lord bestows favor and honor; no good thing does he withhold from those whose walk is blameless. O Lord Almighty, blessed is the man who trusts in You.

Good Morning, God! *You are my sun and shield.* You are the true light of the world. If we walk in Your light, we will stay on the straight path. Lord You bless me daily with Your love and grace. Your blessings flow like showers of warm spring rains. Your goodness covers me with favor. I am truly *blessed because I trust in You.*

Lord Jesus, help me to walk blamelessly. Help me to . . .

GOOD MORNING, GOD!
July 15

2 Chronicles 7:13-15

"When I shut up the heavens so that there is no rain, or command locusts to devour the land or send a plague among my people, if my people who are called by my Name, will humble themselves and pray and seek my face and turn from their wicked ways, then will I hear from heaven and will forgive their sin. Now my eyes will be open and my ears attentive to the prayers offered in this place. . ."

Good Morning, God! Lord, You have blessed this nation beyond our imagination. You call us Your people. Help us to humble ourselves, repent and earnestly pray for Your forgiveness. Heal our land, forgive our sins and bring us back under the safety of Your wing. Let us give you all praise, honor and glory.

Bless me to be a blessing to . . .

GOOD MORNING, GOD!
July 16

Mark 1:10-11

As Jesus was coming up out of the water, He saw heaven being torn open and the Spirit descending on Him like a dove. And a voice came from heaven: "You are My Son, Whom I love, with You I am well pleased."

Good Morning, God! What a glorious sight it must have been to see the *heavens being torn open* and to hear Your mighty voice proclaiming Your pleasure with Your Son. Father God, I long to please You and live my life in Christ's footsteps. Help me to be more Christ-like each day. Help me to live a life that reflects Your love and mercy. Let others see Your light shining brilliantly through me, Your servant.

Let me see with His eyes and love with His heart and . . .

GOOD MORNING, GOD!
July 17

Psalm 33:1-4

Sing joyfully to the Lord, you righteous; it is fitting for the upright to praise him. Praise the Lord with harp; make music to him on the ten-stringed lyre. Sing to him a new song; play skillfully, and shout for joy. For the word of the Lord is right and true; he is faithful in all he does.

Good Morning, God! All praise and glory are Yours, O Lord. I rise up joyfully singing Your praises. These scriptures paint a picture of an orchestra praising You in beautiful harmony for all Your goodness. I want to *sing to him a new song* for You have made me a new creation by Your grace and love. I can rest in You *for the word of the Lord is right and true; he is faithful in all he does.* I will praise You in all I do today.

Lord, I give You praise for . . .

GOOD MORNING, GOD!
July 18

Romans 8:38-39

For I am convinced that neither death nor life, neither angels nor demons, neither the present nor the future, nor any powers, neither height nor depth nor anything else in all creation, will be able to separate us from the love of God that is in Christ Jesus our Lord.

Good Morning, God! I love you, Lord. I am filled with Your joy and peace because I know that nothing can separate me from Your love. Your love has no bounds and it is totally unconditional. No matter how far I stray, You will always woo me back to You. No matter what I do, You love me. That is who You are. You are a God of love and grace. You will love me forever. Thank You, Lord.

Help me today to boldly . . .

GOOD MORNING, GOD!
July 19

Philippians 1:8-11

God can testify how I long for all of you with the affection of Christ Jesus. And this is my prayer: that your love may abound more and more in knowledge and depth of insight, so that you may be able to discern what is best and may be pure and blameless until the day of Christ, filled with the fruit of righteousness that comes through Jesus Christ – to the glory and praise of God.

Good Morning, God! You know I love You and You know that I truly try to live a pure and blameless life. You also know that I fail most of the time. I do pray that I may have *more knowledge and depth of insight to be able to discern* Your will and put it to work in my life. I want to *be filled with the fruit of righteousness that comes through Jesus Christ – to the glory and praise of God.*

Let Your light shine through me so that . . .

GOOD MORNING, GOD!
July 20

Job 5:7-10

Yet man is born to trouble as surely as sparks fly upward. "But if it were I, I would appeal to God; I would lay my cause before Him. He performs wonders that cannot be fathomed, miracles that cannot be counted. He bestows rain on the earth; he sends water upon the countryside."

Good Morning, God! Why do I think that I need to solve all my problems myself? I know You have promised to provide all I need and keep me from harm: *consider the lilies.* I have Your Promises! *You perform wonders that cannot be fathomed, miracles that cannot be counted.* I have personally seen Your wonders and miracles. I have seen Your Majesty in all creation. How can I ever doubt You?

Lord, let me turn my life over to You and . . .

GOOD MORNING, GOD!
July 21

Psalm 98:1-2

Sing to the Lord a new song, for He has done marvelous things; His right hand and His holy arm have worked salvation for Him. The Lord has made His salvation known and revealed His righteousness to the nations.

Good Morning, God! I want to sing a new song to You, Oh Lord. I want to sing of the *salvation* You have prepared for all believers. I want the world to know that *You have done marvelous things.* I want to shout Your praises throughout the land. I want everyone to know what joy it is to be Your child and the peace of knowing we are saved because of Your love for us and the sacrifice of Your Son.

Open a door for me today so that I might . . .

GOOD MORNING, GOD!
July 22

2 Timothy 3:14-17

But as for you, continue in what you have learned and have become convinced of, because you know those from who you learned it, and how from infancy you have known the holy Scriptures, which are able to make you wise for salvation through faith in Christ Jesus. All Scripture is God-breathed and is useful for teaching, rebuking, correcting and training in righteousness, so that the man of God may be thoroughly equipped for every good work.

Good Morning, God! I love to spend my quite-time in the morning relishing every word from Your Scripture. I know these are Your Words directly to me. You speak to me through Your Scripture and I delight in every way. I love the sweet communion we have through reading Your Word. I want to grow in knowledge of Your Word because that is how I know You and how very much You love me.

Open my eyes so . . .

GOOD MORNING, GOD!
July 23

Jude 1:1-2

To those who have been called, who are loved by God the Father and kept by Jesus Christ: Mercy, peace and love be yours in abundance.

Good Morning, God! What a glorious inheritance we have as Your children! What love You have lavished on me that, first of all, You called me to serve You, but also that *You keep me in Jesus Christ* and offer to me Your *mercy, peace and love in abundance.* You are truly an Awesome God! *I am loved by God the Father and kept by Jesus Christ.* That is truly the greatest blessing of all. Thank You, Lord!

I love you, Lord, and today I will . . .

GOOD MORNING, GOD!
July 24

Psalm 103:1-3

Praise the Lord, O my soul; all my inmost being praise His holy name. Praise the Lord, O my soul, and forget not all His benefits – who forgives all your sins and heals all your diseases. Blessed are they who maintain justice, who constantly do what is right.

Good Morning, God! Lord, my heart overflows with Your goodness and there is so much for which to praise You. You are a great and loving God. You say You will never leave us nor forsake us. You are there guiding us and, when the way becomes too treacherous, You even carry us. You *forgive all our sins and heal all our diseases.* Thank You, Lord, for loving me. I will *praise the Lord and with all my inmost being praise His holy name.* Glory to God!

I will serve You today by . . .

GOOD MORNING, GOD!
July 25

John 3:16-17

For God so loved the world that He gave His one and only Son, that whoever believes in Him shall not perish but have eternal life. For God did not send His Son into the world to condemn the world, but to save the world through Him.

Good Morning, God! O what a glorious promise. I know I am loved and saved by the Lord of the Universe. You love every person on this earth to the point that You were willing to sacrifice Your one and only Son to suffer and die that we might be saved. Your great love is the motivation behind His excruciating death for us. His great love for us and His sacrifice offer me an eternal life with You in heaven. Thank You, Lord Jesus for loving me that much.

Help me to show that love by . . .

GOOD MORNING, GOD!
July 26

1 Timothy 1: 15-16

Here is a trustworthy saying that deserves full acceptance: Christ Jesus came into the world to save sinners – of whom I am the worst. But for that very reason I was shown mercy so that in me, the worst of sinners, Christ Jesus might display His unlimited patience as an example for those who would believe on Him and receive eternal life.

Good Morning, God! When I read that Paul considered himself the worst of sinners, I am humbled beyond measure. I know that I am the one worthy of that title but *You have shown me mercy* and given me eternal life. *Christ Jesus came into the world to save sinners.* Thank you for Your *unlimited patience for those who would believe.* I am overwhelmed by Your great mercy and grace. Thank you, Lord Jesus.

Today, let me be worthy of Your mercy as I . . .

GOOD MORNING, GOD!
July 27

Jeremiah 29:11

"For I know the plans I have for you," declares the Lord, "plans to prosper you and not to harm you, plans to give you hope and a future."

Good Morning, God! What glorious words are these, that You have plans for me to prosper. I am part of Your plan. You have a purpose for every person on this earth. I strive daily to be a better Christian and to serve You with my whole heart. I want to share Your Good News with everyone. Thank you for giving me *hope and a future.* I know that no matter how difficult my path may be, I will spend eternity with You. That is all that matters and I am filled with joy.

Show me how to share this good news with . . .

GOOD MORNING, GOD!
July 28

James 1:2-5

Consider it pure joy, my brothers, whenever you face trials of many kinds, because you know that the testing of your faith develops perseverance. Perseverance must finish its work so that you may be mature and complete, not lacking anything. If any of you lacks wisdom, he should ask God, who gives generously to all without finding fault, and it will be given to him.

Good Morning, God! It's not easy when we are facing trials in this life. They can be so encompassing as to strangle the hope and joy out of us. Help me to remember that it is through these trials that my faith is strengthened and I'm a stronger Christian. I want to become *mature and complete, not lacking anything.* I do *ask for wisdom* to know You better and love You more so that I can accomplish the good works You have planned for me.

When I encounter trials, help me to . . .

GOOD MORNING, GOD!
July 29

Revelation 3:15-16

I know your deeds, that you are neither cold nor hot. I wish you were either one or the other! So, because you are lukewarm – neither hot nor cold – I am about to spit you out of my mouth.

Good Morning, God! This scripture scares me to death. I love You with all my heart but I get so caught up in the world. I'm afraid I take You and Your mercy for granted. I want to be so close to You that I can feel the warmth of Your love. Don't let me disappoint You by being lukewarm. Set me on fire for You. Let me be a blazing hot coal of Your love and mercy. Let others feel Your warmth and goodness through me.

Let me shine for You so that . . .

GOOD MORNING, GOD!
July 30

Colossians 2:6-8

So then, just as you received Christ Jesus as Lord, continue to live in him, rooted and built up in him, strengthened in the faith as you were taught, and overflowing with thankfulness. See to it that no one takes you captive through hollow and deceptive philosophy, which depends on human tradition rather than on Christ.

Good Morning, God! I am truly *overflowing with thankfulness.* I am so blessed to know You and love You. I am so thankful You have given me Your Spirit to strengthen my faith. I want to live in You and want You to live through me. Help me to be faithful to all Your teachings. Do not let me be deceived with the *philosophy* of this world but lean only on *Christ.*

I am especially thankful for . . .

GOOD MORNING, GOD!
July 31

Hebrews 11:1-2

Now faith is being sure of what we hope for and certain of what we do not see. By faith we understand that the universe was formed at God's command, so that what is seen was not made out of what was visible.

Good Morning, God! What incredible Words these are. I am so sure of my salvation that I can live each day joyously waiting for Your return. I love my life and I am truly blessed, but knowing that I am Your child gives me hope for the future. Even though I can't see You, I feel Your presence. Lord, I want everyone to be this secure and joyful in their faith. This is Your true peace.

Help me to proclaim Your peace so that . . .

August

GOOD MORNING, GOD!
August 1

2 Thessalonians 1:11-12

> *With this in mind, we constantly pray for you, that our God may count you worthy of His calling and that by His power He may fulfill every good purpose of yours and every act prompted by your faith. We pray this so that the name of our Lord Jesus may be glorified in you and you in Him, according to the grace of our God and the Lord Jesus Christ.*

Good Morning, God! Oh what a wonder that You could use someone as unworthy as me to *fulfill Your good purpose.* Thank You for trusting me with this great mission. It is only through the power of Your Holy Spirit and through *the grace of our God and the Lord Jesus Christ* that I am able to serve You. I thank You for Your calling and I pray that everything I do this day will bring You glory.

Holy Spirit, guide me to . . .

GOOD MORNING, GOD!
August 2

Jeremiah 9:23-24

This is what the LORD says: "Let not the wise boast of their wisdom or the strong boast of their strength or the rich boast of their riches, but let the one who boasts boast about this: that they have the understanding to know me, that I am the LORD, who exercises kindness, justice and righteousness on earth, for in these I delight," declares the LORD.

Good Morning, God! O God, in Whom can I boast other than in You? Everything I have is from You. I am so thankful that You *delight in making Yourself known to me.* I want to know You better and love You more. I am so thankful for Your *kindness, justice and righteousness.* What a wretch I would be without Your love and mercy. You are a glorious God Who delights in showing goodness and mercy to His children.

Lord, I am especially thankful for . . .

GOOD MORNING, GOD!
August 3

Deuteronomy 28:13-14

The LORD will make you the head, not the tail. If you pay attention to the commands of the LORD your God that I give you this day and carefully follow them, you will always be at the top, never at the bottom. Do not turn aside from any of the commands I give you today, to the right or to the left, following other gods and serving them.

Good Morning, God! I love You, Lord. How comforting it is to know that I am Your child and that You will always protect me. You will make me prosper and I will *always be on top.* Help me to follow Your path today and *not turn aside from any of Your commands.* Help me to not let the *other gods* of this world blind me from You and Your love. Show me Your will for my life and let me follow You.

Today I want to serve You by . . .

GOOD MORNING, GOD!
August 4

Matthew 28:18-19

Then Jesus came to them and said, "All authority in heaven and on earth has been given to me. Therefore go and make disciples of all nations, baptizing them in the name of the Father and of the Son and of the Holy Spirit."

Good Morning, God! Lord, this is Your Great Commission to all Your children. Because I am washed by the blood of Jesus and saved from all my sins to spend eternity with You, I must go forth and tell everyone about You and Your Good News. I am so blessed I must share this message of Your love and the news of Your redemption for all who believe. Let Your Spirit burn in me and give me the courage and the wisdom to *go and make disciples.*

Use me to . . .

GOOD MORNING, GOD!
August 5

Proverbs 16:23-24

A wise man's heart guides his mouth, and his lips promote instruction. Pleasant words are a honeycomb sweet to the soul and healing to the bones.

Good Morning, God! I hate myself when I let my tongue get the best of me and say things I can never take back. I know that my words have the power as of a rudder on a ship. They are very small but can have a huge impact. I pray that You will guard my words today and let them be only uplifting. Let my words be Your Words. Let them build up and encourage. Let Your Spirit burn within me so that Your love overflows through me to everyone I encounter today.

Lord, inspire me to . . .

GOOD MORNING, GOD!
August 6

Matthew 25:37-40

"Then the righteous will answer him, 'Lord, when did we see you hungry and feed you, or thirsty and give you something to drink? When did we see you a stranger and invite you in, or needing clothes and clothe you? When did we see you sick or in prison and go to visit you?'" The King will reply, "I tell you the truth, whatever you did for one of the least of these brothers of mine, you did for me."

Good Morning, God! Help me to see everyone as a precious child of God. Help me to look past the outward appearance to the heart as You do. Let me not be timid about stepping out in faith to do something to help those in need. Let me be the hands and feet of Christ for those who need You. Use me to nurture and love and not to judge. Show me what I can do for *the least of these brothers of Yours.*

Most of all, use me to . . .

GOOD MORNING, GOD!
August 7

Romans 5:1-2

Therefore, since we have been justified through faith, we have peace with God through our Lord Jesus Christ, through whom we have gained access by faith into this grace in which we now stand. And we rejoice in the hope of the glory of God.

Good Morning, God! I can't imagine getting up and facing a day without knowing of Your love and grace. My life would be in shambles with worry, regret, apprehension and great fear. But, thank You, Lord, for the peace that You give to me each day *through our Lord Jesus Christ.* The Peace of Christ sustains me and brings me great joy. The world has nothing to hurl at me that You can't overcome. Thank You, Lord. I *rejoice in the hope of the glory of God.*

Let me rejoice in Your glory today by . . .

GOOD MORNING, GOD!
August 8

1 Timothy 6:6-8

But godliness with contentment is great gain. For we brought nothing into this world, and we can take nothing out of it. But if we have food and clothing, we will be content with that.

Good Morning, God! I am so content. I can achieve nothing on my own. You provide everything we need. You abundantly give us more than we need. You give us not only the necessities of food, shelter and security, but we are surrounded by the majesty and beauty of the world from the mountains to the tiniest humming bird. You have gone to great lengths to bring us joy and pleasure. I am content resting in Your abounding goodness and grace for a sinner such as I.

Help me to find joy in even the . . .

GOOD MORNING, GOD!
August 9

Philippians 4:4-6

Rejoice in the Lord always, I will say it again: Rejoice! Let your gentleness be evident to all. The Lord is near. Do not be anxious about anything, but in everything, by prayer and petition, with thanksgiving, present your request to God.

Good Morning, God! Sometimes I don't even know how to pray, but You know my requests before I even ask them. I rejoice in knowing that You are near and I can bring any and everything to you. You say *in everything present your requests to God* – nothing is too great or too small. I know that You hear my prayers. I know they will be answered according to Your will. I pray with thanksgiving because I know You are my God and my prayers are important to You. Thank You, Lord.

Help me not to be anxious about . . .

GOOD MORNING, GOD!
August 10

Acts 1:8

"But you will receive power when the Holy Spirit comes on you; and you will be my witnesses in Jerusalem, and all Judea and Samaria, and to the ends of the earth."

Good Morning, God! Thank You for the gift of Your Holy Spirit to live in me. Help me to know the power of Your Spirit within me. Let me feel the fire burning inside me. Help me to empty myself of me and be a vessel for Your Spirit to flow. You say that *when the Spirit comes we can do even greater things than You.* I know this is only possible through the power I receive from You. I am thankful You can use me to further Your Kingdom and be Your witness.

Let today be a day that I can . . .

GOOD MORNING, GOD!
August 11

John 15:7-10

"If you remain in me and my words remain in you, ask whatever you wish, and it will be given you. This is to my Father's glory that you bear much fruit, showing yourselves to be my disciples. As the Father has loved me, so have I loved you. Now remain in my love. If you obey my commands, you will remain in my love, just as I have obeyed my Father's commands and remain in his love."

Good Morning, God! I want everything I do to bring You glory. Help me to *obey your commands and remain in your love.* I want to *bear abundant fruit so that everyone will know that I am Your disciple.* And now You say that *if I remain in Your words, whatever I wish will be given to me.* This is more than I can comprehend. You are truly an Awesome God! Thank You, Lord.

Lord, today I want people to know I'm Your disciple when I . . .

GOOD MORNING, GOD!
August 12

Luke 21:14-15

But make up your mind not to worry beforehand how you will defend yourselves. For I will give you words and wisdom that none of your adversaries will be able to resist or contradict.

Good Morning, God! I never cease to be amazed at Your power and glory. You promise to *give me the words when I don't know what to say.* You have created me to be Your witness and disciple. You will even give me words that will move the hearts of those to whom I witness. How can I *worry beforehand how I will defend myself?* I *will make up my mind* to be Your witness and share Your Word with everyone. All glory, honor and praise to You, O God!

Give me those words in order to . . .

GOOD MORNING, GOD!
August 13

2 Chronicles 26: 1, 5

Then all the people of Judah took Uzziah, who was sixteen years old, and made him king in place of his father Amaziah. He sought God during the days of Zechariah, who instructed him in the fear of God. As long as he sought the Lord, God gave him success.

Good Morning, God! Help me to realize that this day is for Your glory. I long to know Your will and accomplish what You have set out for me today. It isn't up to what I can do, but what You can do through me. Without You I can do nothing. I can do exceedingly greater things when I trust You and follow You. As long as I seek You, You will make all that I do be successful for Your Kingdom. Praise God!

Thank you, Dear God, for being with me today and help me to . . .

GOOD MORNING, GOD!
August 14

Psalm 27:6-8

Then my head will be exalted above the enemies who surround me; at his tabernacle will I sacrifice with shouts of joy; I will sing and make music to the Lord. Hear my voice when I call, O Lord; be merciful to me and answer me. My heart says of You, "Seek His face!" Your face, Lord, I will seek.

Good Morning, God! I know that when I have trials in this life all I need is to *seek Your face. I want to sing and make music to the Lord.* I need to call upon Your Name to rescue me and *be merciful and answer me.* You are always there, but I get so caught up in the tsunami of the world around me that I forget. You alone can calm the storm in my soul. *Your face, Lord, I will seek.*

Thank You for being in control of my life. Let me always remember to . . .

GOOD MORNING, GOD!
August 15

Daniel 9:17-18

"Now, our God, hear the prayers and petitions of your servant. For your sake, O Lord, look with favor on your desolate sanctuary. Give ear, O God and hear; . . . We do not make requests of You because we are righteous, but because of Your great mercy. . ."

Good Morning, God! I come to You each day with myriads of problems. I ask You each day to *hear the prayers and petitions of your servant..* You are my strength and shield. I know that *all things are possible through You.* I also know that I am not worthy. I know that You answer my prayers, not because of what or who I am, but because of *Your great mercy.*

Lord God, thank You for loving me, the sinner I am, and help me to . . .

GOOD MORNING, GOD!
August 16

Matthew 16:26-27

What good will it be for a man if he gains the whole world, yet forfeits his soul? Or what can a man give in exchange for his soul? For the Son of Man is going to come in his Father's glory with his angels and then he will reward each person according to what he has done.

Good Morning, God! You know I have a lot on my plate, Lord. I get up early and go to bed late. I keep my nose to the grindstone all day. I rush; I worry; I get frustrated; I get angry; I get discouraged; I let myself become so overwhelmed with all this STUFF. Let me stop and praise You. Let me pray without ceasing. Let me keep You close to me throughout the day. Lord, please don't let Satan steal my joy in You.

My life belongs to You, Sweet Jesus. Help me to remember that so that I can . . .

GOOD MORNING, GOD!
August 17

Romans 12: 1-2a

Therefore, I urge you, brothers, in view of God's mercy, to offer your bodies as living sacrifices, holy and pleasing to God – this is your spiritual act of worship. Do not conform any longer to the pattern of this world, but be transformed by the renewing of your mind.

Good Morning, God! Lord, Your mercy abounds. You have given Yourself as a ransom for me. I am a child of the Most High God. I have Your Spirit within me. Lord, let me *offer my body as a living sacrifice, holy and pleasing to* You. I want to please You, Lord. Let me not *be conformed any longer to the pattern of this world.* Let me live according to Your will. Let me *be transformed by the renewing of my mind.* Open my heart and soul to be more Christ like. Let my life be a witness and testimony of Your love and grace.

Let others see Your light in me so that . . .

GOOD MORNING, GOD!
August 18

Exodus 15:15b-18

> *. . . The people of Canaan will melt away; terror and dread will fall upon them. By the power of Your arm they will be as still as a stone until Your people pass by, O Lord, until the people You bought pass by. You will bring them in and plant them on the mountain of your inheritance – the place, O Lord, you made for your dwelling, the sanctuary, O Lord, your hands established. The Lord will reign for ever and ever.*

Good Morning, God! What a Mighty God we serve. What joy it is to know that *the power of Your* arm covers me in every situation and circumstance I encounter. The enemy is lurking, *seeking whom he may devour*, but the *power of Your strong arm* fills him with terror and dread. I am Yours -- You bought me with Your blood.

Lord, because I know You are with me, give me confidence today to . . .

GOOD MORNING, GOD!
August 19

1 Kings 20:11, 13

> *The king of Israel answered, "Tell him: 'One who puts on his armor should not boast like one who takes it off.'" Meanwhile a prophet came to Ahab king of Israel and announced, "This is what the Lord says: 'Do you see this vast army? I will give it into your hand today, and then you will know that I am the Lord.'"*

Good Morning, God! God of wonder and God of might, You have promised to deliver me from the *vast armies of this world*. What shall I fear? You have promised to *deliver my enemies into my hand*. Lord, I can't wait to watch You work in my life today. I will give You all the glory. I *know that You are the Lord.*

Lord, help me to know that it is You and not me, so I have confidence to . . .

GOOD MORNING, GOD!
August 20

Romans 2:1-3

You, therefore, have no excuse, you who pass judgment on someone else, for at whatever point you judge the other, you are condemning yourself, because you who pass judgment do the same things. Now we know that God's judgment against those who do such things is based on truth. So when you, a mere man, pass judgment on them and yet do the same things, do you think you will escape God's judgment?

Good Morning, God! I know that judging others is one of my greatest sins. You tell me *I have no excuse* because *I do the same things* and I know I do. It is so much easier to see the sins of others than my own. I pray that You help me not to judge others but to see them through Your eyes. You alone are the judge. Help me to show Your love and compassion to all God's children.

Let me see as You see, Sweet Jesus, so that I can . . .

GOOD MORNING, GOD!
August 21

James 1:19-21

My dear brothers, take note of this: Everyone should be quick to listen, slow to speak and slow to become angry, for man's anger does not bring about the righteous life that God desires. Therefore, get rid of all moral filth and the evil that is so prevalent and humbly accept the word planted in you, which can save you.

Good Morning, God! The words of James are so full of wisdom for our life. Let me *be quick to listen, slow to speak and slow to become angry.* Help me to take these words to heart and keep them in my mind as I go through the day. Let everything I say bring You glory. Don't let Satan get a foothold in any aspect of my day. Help me to have *the righteous life You desire for me.*

Lord, help me to listen as You would listen so I can . . .

GOOD MORNING, GOD!
August 22

2 Samuel 22:1-3a

David sang to the Lord the words of this song when the Lord delivered him from the hand of all his enemies and from the hand of Saul. He said: "The Lord is my rock, my fortress and my deliverer; my God is my rock, in whom I take refuge, my shield and the horn of my salvation. . ."

Good Morning, God! Lord, I sing Your praise each and every morning. I know that You will be with me throughout the day. You **are** *my rock; my deliverer* and my God. *I can take refuge in You* no matter what is going on around me. You keep me from the path of Satan's fiery arrows. You are the God in *whom I take refuge, my shield and the horn of my salvation.*

Lord, refuge is such a beautiful word. Help me to . . .

GOOD MORNING, GOD!
August 23

Joshua 3:7, 9-10a

And the Lord said to Joshua, "Today I will begin to exalt you in the eyes of all Israel, so they may know that I am with you as I was with Moses." Joshua said to the Israelites, "Come here and listen to the words of the Lord your God. This is how you will know that the living God is among you. . ."

Good Morning, God! You have performed miracle after miracle among Your people. You parted the Red Sea; You provided manna; You provided a cloud by day and a fiery pillar by night. You have always shown us that *You are among us* guiding and caring for us. Help me to *listen to the words of the Lord my God.* Let me hear these words and never forget that You are with me. Thank You, Lord.

Help me to listen to Your Words for . . .

GOOD MORNING, GOD!
August 24

Exodus 4:10-12

Moses said to the Lord, "O Lord, I have never been eloquent, neither in the past nor since you have spoken to your servant. I am slow of speech and tongue." The Lord said to him [Moses], "Who gave man his mouth? Who makes him deaf or mute? Who gives him sight or makes him blind? Is it not I, the Lord? Now go; I will help you speak and will teach you what to say."

Good Morning, God! Oh, Lord, what an awesome command. What an awesome promise. Even when I don't know what to say, You will *help me speak and teach me what to say.* I'm not worthy to speak Your Word, but through the power of Your Holy Spirit You can use me. You have called me and will equip me. How can I not shout the Good News!

Lord, relieve my fears to witness and let Your Spirit guide me to . . .

GOOD MORNING, GOD!
August 25

Jeremiah 30:21-22

"Their leader will be one of their own; their ruler will arise from among them. I will bring him near and he will come close to me, for who is he who will devote himself to be close to me, declares the Lord. So you will be my people, and I will be your God."

Good Morning, God! What a beautiful picture of our Savior. You will *bring him near and he will come close to You.* What a glorious plan You have for our salvation. *We are Your people and You are our God.* What an incredible blessing. It sounds so simple but we have to realize the price You paid. You sacrificed Your Son. Without Him we couldn't be Your children. Thank You for *being my God and allowing me to be Your child.*

Lord God, show me how I can glorify you today by . . .

GOOD MORNING, GOD!
August 26

Revelation 21:3-4

And I heard a loud voice from the throne saying, "Now the dwelling of God is with men, and He will live with them. They will be His people, and God Himself will be with them and be their God. He will wipe every tear from their eyes. There will be no more death or mourning or crying or pain, for the old order of things has passed away. . ."

Good Morning, God! Oh God, Your promise is what we long for. Can you imagine, **"a *loud voice from the throne*"?** What will it be like to dwell in Your presence for eternity? *You will wipe every tear from their eyes.* There will be no more sorrow or pain and suffering. We know we can't comprehend what Heaven will be like, but just knowing that we will be with You gives us hope and total peace and joy.

Precious Savior, give me the words to let others know that . . .

GOOD MORNING, GOD!
August 27

Matthew 5:14-16

"You are the light of the world. A city on a hill cannot be hidden. Neither do people light a lamp and put it under a bowl. Instead they put it on its stand and it gives light to everyone in the house. In the same way, let your light shine before men, that they may see your good deeds and praise your Father in heaven."

Good Morning, God! *You are the light of the world.* The only light I have is from You. Fill me with Your love and your light. Put me to work for You. Help me to light Your world so that everyone can see You in all that I do. Let me be an example of your love and mercy. *Let my light shine before men, that they may see your good deeds and praise your Father in heaven.* All praise and glory to Your, O Lord.

Lord, let everything I do bring glory to You and . . .

GOOD MORNING, GOD!
August 28

Matthew 16:24-25

Then Jesus said to his disciples, "If anyone would come after me, he must deny himself and take up his cross and follow me. For whoever wants to save his life will lose it, but whoever loses his life for me will find it."

Good Morning, God! I want to fill my life with You today. I want to spend every minute of this day knowing that You are right by my side guiding the steps in my journey closer and closer to you. Help me to cast off the things of this world and *take up Your cross and follow You,* for in doing so I will be filled with Your joy and peace. Let me *lose my life for You and I will find it.* Let me know that You are all that is important in this world. Thank You, Lord.

Lord, let me let go of the dross in my life so that I can *come after You* to . . .

GOOD MORNING, GOD!
August 29

Matthew 17:18-21

Jesus rebuked the demon and it came out of the boy, and he was healed from that moment. Then the disciples came to Jesus in private and asked, "Why couldn't we drive it out?" He replied, "Because you have so little faith, I tell you the truth, if you have faith as small as a mustard seed, you can say to this mountain, 'Move from here to there' and it will move. Nothing will be impossible for you."

Good Morning, God! Lord, I love Your promises. You tell me that *nothing will be impossible if I have faith in You. If I have faith as small as a mustard seed I can move mountains.* I am claiming that promise and I know that You will never forsake me. No matter what this day holds, I have faith that You will be in control. You make all things new and right. Thank You for being my Lord and King.

Precious Savior, increase my faith so that I can . . .

GOOD MORNING, GOD!
August 30

Romans 8:30-32

And those he predestined, he also called; those he called he also justified, he also glorified. What, then, shall we say in response to this? If God is for us, who can be against us? He who did not spare his own Son, but gave him up for us all —how will he not also, along with him, graciously give us all things?

Good Morning, God! O Lord, how can I even worry about my life and all that is going on around me? You have *predestined me to be called to be Your child*. You do not force me to be Yours, but You love me so much that You gave Your only Son for me. Through Him I am *justified and glorified* as a child of God. You are on my side and anyone against me doesn't stand a chance! How awesome that is. Not only that, but You *graciously give us all things*. Help me to remember this as I try to give my all for You today.

Knowing that You are for me, help me to . . .

GOOD MORNING, GOD!
August 31

1 Timothy 2:1-4

I urge, then, first of all, that requests, prayers, intercession and thanksgiving be made for everyone — for kings and all those in authority, that we may live peaceful and quiet lives in all godliness and holiness. This is good, and pleases God our Savior, who wants all men to be saved and to come to knowledge of the truth.

Good Morning, God! This world is in such turmoil and strife. That is all we see and read about in the news. You tell us that we are to pray for all in authority and that it pleases You. Let us *live peaceful and quiet live in all godliness and holiness.* Lord, I earnestly pray for all the world leaders that they may know Your truth and bring peace to Your land. We want to please You, Lord.

Give me Your *knowledge of the truth* and help me to . . .

$$\text{\maltese} \quad \text{\maltese} \quad \text{\maltese}$$

September

GOOD MORNING, GOD!
September 1

1 Peter 3:8-9

Finally, all of you, live in harmony with one another; be sympathetic, love as brothers, be compassionate and humble. Do not repay evil with evil or insult with insult, but with blessing, because to this you were called so that you may inherit a blessing.

Good Morning, God! This is a tall order, Lord. I do truly want to live in harmony with everyone, but it isn't as easy as it sounds. I let my pride get in the way and want to let them know they have hurt me and get back at them. You ask me to be a blessing and I know that is the right thing to do. Keep Satan behind me so that I'm not tempted *to repay evil for evil.* Help me to be more like Jesus and show nothing but love and kindness and we will both *inherit a blessing.*

Lord, You have called me to be a blessing. Show me how I can . . .

GOOD MORNING, GOD!
September 2

Isaiah 25:9

He will swallow up death forever. The Sovereign Lord will wipe away the tears from all faces; he will remove the disgrace of his people from all the earth. The Lord has spoken. In that day they will say, "Surely this is our God; we trusted in him, and he saved us. This is the Lord we trusted in him; let us rejoice and be glad in his salvation."

Good Morning, God! Let these verses ring through my ears and heart all this day long. Let me know that no matter what I may face today, You are my God and I will *trust in You*. You love me so much that You have offered me the gift of Your Son for my salvation. I am a child of the Most High God. I will *rejoice and be glad in Your salvation*. Let everyone I encounter see Your light and love shining through me. All praise and glory are Yours.

Lord, help me to trust in You so that . . .

GOOD MORNING, GOD!
September 3

Genesis 28:15-16

I am with you and will watch over you wherever you go, and I will not leave you until I have done what I have promised you. When Jacob awoke from his sleep, he thought, "Surely the Lord is in this place, and I was not aware of it."

Good Morning, God! How awesome it is to know that *you will watch over me and not leave me*. You have promised. Thank You, Precious Savior. Let me always be aware of Your Word and that *You are always in this place* no matter where I am, You've been there before me. You know what I am going through better than I. Please don't let me take You for granted. Let me ever give You thanks and praise for Your loving kindness to me.

Lord, let me go through this day knowing that You are *in this place* and will . . .

GOOD MORNING, GOD!
September 4

Proverbs 3:5-6

Trust in the Lord with all your heart. And lean not on your own understanding; in all your ways acknowledge Him, and He shall direct your paths.

Good Morning, God! Oh, Lord, I want to trust You with all my heart. I know You promise to *never leave me nor forsake me,* but sometimes it is hard to just let go and let You be in control. It seems that I should be able to "fix" my life. But, Lord, You tell me in Your Word *not to lean on my understanding,* but to trust my life to You and *You will direct my paths.* Help me to believe this truth and follow You as You direct me in the path You would have me go and I will give You all the glory!

Lord, let me lean on You today to . . .

GOOD MORNING, GOD!
September 5

Psalm 19:9-13

The fear of the Lord is pure, enduring forever. The ordinances of the Lord are sure and altogether righteous. They are more precious than gold, than much pure gold; they are sweeter than honey, than honey from the comb. By them is your servant warned, in keeping them there is great reward. Who can discern his errors? Forgive my hidden faults. Keep your servant also from willful sins, may they not rule over me. Then will I be blameless, innocent of great transgression.

Good Morning, God! Oh Lord, I know I am a wretched sinner. I can't even imagine how many sins I commit that I don't even realize, much less the ones I know I do. I feel like Paul when he says *what he wants to do he doesn't do and what he doesn't want to do he does.* I confess my sins to you and then turn right around and do the same thing. Help me to see my sins and realize that I grieve You when I continue living this way.

Holy Spirit, convict me and help me to be . . .

GOOD MORNING, GOD!
September 6

Ephesians 2:4-5

But because of his great love for us, God, who is rich in mercy, made us alive with Christ even when we were dead in transgressions – it is by grace you have been saved. And God raised us up with Christ and seated us with him in the heavenly realms in Christ Jesus.

Good Morning, God! Glorious Father, You are so full of grace and mercy. It makes my heart sing to know that You love me so much that You sent Your Son to wash my sins as white as snow. You have lifted the weight of my sins from me and placed them on my Precious Savior. *The wages of sin is death,* and You have removed that sentence from me and will *raise me up and I'll be seated with Him in the heavenly realms.* Thank you, Jesus, for making me free from the slavery of my sins.

Lord, let me show you my praise today by . . .

GOOD MORNING, GOD!
September 7

Psalm 89:8-9

O Lord God Almighty, who is like you? You are mighty, O Lord, and your faithfulness surrounds you. You rule over the surging sea; when its waves mount up, you still them.

Good Morning, God! When I read Your Word and hear of Your glory and might, I am in awe of You. How is it that the God of the universe knows me by name and loves me? You are my Jehovah Jireh, the God Who provides. How can I let myself worry about the things of this world when Your love can calm all the storms in my life. You reign over the world and in me. You can rebuke the winds and the sea. There is none greater than You and You love me. How awesome is that?

Lord, let me keep You first in my life today so that I . . .

GOOD MORNING, GOD!
September 8

Proverbs 2:1-5

My son, if you accept my words and store up my commands within you, turning your ear to wisdom and applying your heart to understanding, and if you call out for insight and cry aloud for understanding, and if you look for it as for silver and search for it as for hidden treasure, then you will understand the fear of the Lord and find the knowledge of God.

Good Morning, God! Lord, I spend so much time praying to know Your will for my life. I love You and my deepest desire is to live my life for you. Your Word gives me the answer I've been searching for. If I seek You with my whole heart and hunger and thirst for You, Your Spirit will open the eyes of my heart and I will truly *find the knowledge of God*. I don't have to search any longer. You will reveal it to me as I grow in my faith walk.

Lord, help me to know You better and . . .

GOOD MORNING, GOD!
September 9

Mark 8:34-36

Then he called the crowd to him along with his disciples and said: "If anyone would come after me, he must deny himself and take up his cross and follow me. For whoever wants to save his life will lose it, but whoever loses his life for me and for the gospel will save it. What good is it for a man to gain the whole world, yet forfeit his soul?"

Good Morning, God! Lord, I consider it my greatest joy and privilege to follow You. I will *take up my cross and follow You*. The things that were once so valuable to me are now merely rubbish – things that I made my idols and kept me from seeing You clearly. I want to serve You all my days. I want others to know You and know the joy it is to know that we will spend eternity singing Your praises and worshiping You.

Lord, let Your Spirit burn within me so that I can . . .

GOOD MORNING, GOD!
September 10

Romans 8:33-35

Who will bring any charge against those whom God has chosen? It is God who justifies. Who is he that condemns? Christ Jesus, who died – more than that, who was raised to life – is at the right hand of God and is also interceding for us. Who shall separate us from the love of Christ?

Good Morning, God! What a joy it is to know that I am a child of God – the God Who did not spare His Son, but gave Him to take away my sins. A *chosen* child of God for whom *our Lord and Savior is making intercession.* What great love is that? It is beyond my imagination that You could love me so much that you would pray for me. And even better yet, *who shall separate us from the love of Christ?* Thank You, Lord, Jesus.

Lord, let me show that same love to others by . . .

GOOD MORNING, GOD!
September11

Psalm 27: 1-3

The Lord is my light and my salvation – whom shall I fear? The Lord is the stronghold of my life – of whom shall I be afraid? The evil men advance against me to devour my flesh, when my enemies and my foes attack me, my heart will not fear; even though war break out against me, even then I will be confident.

Good Morning, God! David was a *man after Your own heart,* but his life was filled with trouble and conflict. He was constantly under attack from either Saul or other foes, yet he knew in Whom he could trust. Lord, I give You thanks and praise that You are the Sovereign God of this world and You are in control of all things. Help me to always see that and not become distressed when I seem to be surrounded by evil. *Even though war break out against me, even then I will be confident.*

Lord, let my trust in You grow to the point that . . .

GOOD MORNING, GOD!
September 12

Hebrews 3: 1-2

Therefore, holy brothers, who share in the heavenly calling, fix your thoughts on Jesus, the apostle and high priest whom we confess. He was faithful to the one who anointed him, just as Moses was faithful in all God's house.

Good Morning, God! Lord, we are all called to share the good news and bring You glory. I pray that Your Spirit will burn in me and *fix my thoughts on Jesus*, so that I can be the vessel through whom You speak. When I don't have the words, Your Spirit within me will tell me what to say. Let my words be Your words. Let Your light shine through me so that everyone can see You and Your faithfulness to save and redeem us all.

Lord, I give You thanks and praise for . . .

GOOD MORNING, GOD!
September 13

John 6: 39-40

This is the will of Him who sent Me, that I shall lose none of all those He has given Me, but raise them up at the last day. For My Father's will is that everyone who looks to the Son and believes in Him shall have eternal life, and I will raise them up at the last day.

Good Morning, God! Dear Jesus, what a glorious promise. Nothing can separate me from Your love and mercy and grace. When I feel so unworthy because of all my sins, You still cherish me and *everyone who looks to the Son and believes in Him shall have eternal life*. Even while Satan is launching his arrows, I have the full armor of God to keep them away. I have You by my side protecting me. Come, Lord Jesus, come. Bring Your Kingdom to this world and let it be filled with Your glory.

Precious Savior, help me to stay in my Father's will and . . .

GOOD MORNING, GOD!
September 14

Psalm 147:1-4

Praise the Lord. How good it is to sing praises to our God, how pleasant and fitting to praise him? The Lord builds up Jerusalem; he gathers the exiles of Israel. He heals the brokenhearted and binds up their wounds. He determines the number of stars and calls them each by name. Great is our Lord and mighty in power; his understanding has no limit.

Good Morning, God! *How good it is to sing praises to our God!* Lord, I will sing Your praises forever. You are a God of love and mercy. You *heal the brokenhearted and bind their wounds.* You are a God of compassion. You love Your children as a Glorious Loving Father. Even though You *determine the number of stars and call each by name,* You know my name and I am precious in Your sight. I will give You all praise and glory forever.

Let, let me praise You today by . . .

GOOD MORNING, GOD!
September 15

Deuteronomy 8:3

He humbled you, causing you to hunger and then feeding you with manna, which neither you nor your fathers had known, to teach you that man does not live on bread alone but on every word that comes from the mouth of the Lord.

Good Morning, God! Humble me, Oh Lord. Humble me to the point that I realize that none of this world is about me. It is only about Your Precious Son and all that You have done for me. Let me *hunger and thirst* for Your Word. Let me know that even when times seem to be the darkest You alone send forth Your Word and provide more than we could ever need. Let Your Word fill my heart today and let me show others the joy it is to be Your child. *Teach me that man does not live on bread alone but on every word that comes from the mouth of the Lord.*

Lord, help me to . . .

GOOD MORNING, GOD!
September 16

Psalm 25:4-6

Show me your ways, O Lord, teach me your paths; guide me in your truth and teach me, for you are God my Savior, and my hope is in you all day long. Remember, O Lord, your great mercy and love, for they are from of old.

Good Morning, God! As I go through this day, O Lord, help me to always remember that my hope is in You. *Teach me your paths; guide me in your truth and teach me, for you are God my Savior.* Your love and mercy surround me and give me peace. I have nothing to fear because You are by my side. You guide me and teach me to be more like Your Son. I want to have His compassion for Your children. I want to see others as He sees. I want to walk in Your ways. *My hope is in you all day long.*

Let me not be so caught up in myself that I fail to . . .

GOOD MORNING, GOD!
September 17

Mark 1:40-42

A man with leprosy came to him and begged him on his knees, "If you are willing, you can make me clean." Filled with compassion, Jesus reached out his hand and touched the man. "I am willing," he said. "Be clean!" Immediately the leprosy left him and he was cured.

Good Morning, God! Lord, when I consider the wonder of your compassion and mercy I am overwhelmed with love for You. By merely reaching out Your Hand the man with leprosy was immediately healed. Lord, I pray that You will reach out Your hand and heal those who need You. Let them feel the power of Your touch and know that You are the Great Physician. You cure our physical and spiritual body. We need to feel You near us today. Give us Your joy and peace.

Precious Savior, give me total faith in Your healing power so that . . .

GOOD MORNING, GOD!
September 18

Revelation 3:20-21

Here I am! I stand at the door and knock. If anyone hears my voice and opens the door, I will come in and eat with him, and he with me. To him who overcomes, I will give the right to sit with me on my throne, just as I overcame and sat down with my Father on his throne.

Good Morning, God! O Lord, I am overwhelmed by these verses. You truly stand at the door of my heart and You are waiting for me to open the door and receive You. Jesus Christ, the Lord of the universe, the Lamb of God, You are waiting for me! It is that simple. We only have to invite You in. You love us and covet a relationship with us. You love us so much You will *give us the right to sit with You on Your throne.* These words are too awesome for me to comprehend. Your goodness and mercy are flowing over me right now and giving me Your peace. Thank you, Jesus.

Lord, help me to overcome . . .

GOOD MORNING, GOD!
September 19

Romans 16:17-18

I urge you, brothers [and sisters], to watch out for those who cause divisions and put obstacles in your way that are contrary to the teaching you have learned. Keep away from them. For such people are not serving our Lord Christ, but their own appetites. By smooth talk and flattery they deceive the minds of naïve people.

Good Morning, God! This world can be a ferocious lion at times, trying to devour whomever it can with lies and deceit. Help me to always remember the *teaching I have learned* and not get caught in the tempter's snare. Satan is the father of all lies. He does everything he can to lure us away from You. Let my mind be filled with Your Word and let me see his *smooth talk and flattery* for just what it is! I refuse to listen to him. I will follow You, O Lord!

Lord, open my eyes and please remove the obstacle of . . .

GOOD MORNING, GOD!
September 20

James 4:7-8a

Submit yourselves, then, to God. Resist the devil, and he will flee from you. Come near to God and he will come near to you.

Good Morning, God! I need to feel You close to me today, Dear Lord. I do truly submit myself to You. I love You, Lord, and I want to be as close as the disciple whom Jesus loved and lean against Your chest. I want to feel the warmth of Your love all around me. I know Satan is prowling around me just waiting for an opportunity to pounce. I WILL resist him. I WILL draw near to You for I know therein lies my strength to overcome his temptations. Draw me closer, Lord. Fill me with the burning desire to know You better and love You more each day.

Thank you, Precious Savior, for . . .

GOOD MORNING, GOD!
September 21

Luke 11:9-10

So I say to you: Ask and it will be given to you; seek and you will find; knock and the door will be opened to you. For everyone who asks receives; he who seeks finds; and to him who knocks, the door will be opened.

Good Morning, God! What an awesome promise, Sweet Jesus. In the midst of the crazy world spinning around me, all I have to do is stop and seek You and I will find all I could possibly desire or need. I know You love me and want the very best for me. I know You don't always answer my prayers instantly and with the answer I think I want. You know what is best for Your will to be done and to further Your Kingdom. You do truly hear every word I pray and You do answer my prayers. This fills my heart with hope and joy. Nothing can separate me from Your love.

Lord, today I am asking, seeking and knocking for . . .

GOOD MORNING, GOD!
September 22

Psalm 77:11-14

I will remember the deeds of the Lord; yes, I will remember your miracles of long ago. I will meditate on all your works and consider all your mighty deeds. Your ways, O God, are holy. What god is so great as our God? You are the God who performs miracles; you display your power among the peoples.

Good Morning, God! This is how I want to spend my entire day – *I will remember the deeds of the Lord; yes, I will remember your miracles of long ago.* You raised Lazarus from the dead and You continue to perform Your miracles around me every minute of every day. Open my heart and eyes to see Your goodness and *power among the peoples.* Let me know that I have nothing to fear for You are my God. You are my holy and great God! All glory and honor are Yours, Lord.

Lord, when I think of how mighty are your deeds, I want to . . .

GOOD MORNING, GOD!
September 23

Romans 10:9-11

That if you confess with your mouth, "Jesus is Lord," and believe in your heart that God raised him from the dead, you will be saved. For it is with your heart that you believe and are justified, and it is with your mouth that you confess and are saved. As the Scripture says, "Anyone who trusts in him will never be put to shame."

Good Morning, God! Jesus, You are truly *Lord.* You are the Lord of my life and I give myself to You completely. I believe because I can feel You near me and working in me. I can feel You holding me and keeping me from harm and shame. I see Your glory and majesty all around me. I love You with my whole heart. I want to shout it from the rooftop to everyone I encounter. I want them to know *You are the Lord.* You are a mighty Lord and worthy to be praised!

Lord, I want to show You praise by . . .

GOOD MORNING, GOD!
September 24

Habakkuk 3:1-2

Lord, I have heard of your fame; I stand in awe of your deeds, O Lord. Renew them in our day, in our time make them known; in wrath remember mercy.

Good Morning, God! Father God, it seems that each day we fall farther and farther away from You. The world is out of control with sin and idolatry. We are spiraling deeper and deeper into despair. We need You, Lord. We need to be reminded of Your awesome love and mercy. We need to remember Your goodness and grace. Let Your Spirit burn within us so that we can be renewed. God, we need You to bless us and keep us close to You. Have mercy on us, O God, and show us Your glory. Let us see what a mighty God You are and seek to do Your will in our lives.

Bring us back to You, O Lord, and . . .

GOOD MORNING, GOD!
September 25

John 1:1-3

In the beginning was the Word, and the Word was with God, and the Word was God. He was with God in the beginning. Through him all things were made; without him nothing was made that has been made.

Good Morning, God! What a beautiful way to start the day – knowing that You are in this world. Your Spirit is living in me. Whom or what shall I fear? You are the Lord of all and the Savior of the universe. Thank You for such love as to die for me – the lowly sinner I am. I love You, Lord, and want to spend the entire day feeling Your presence. Let Your Holy Spirit fill me to overflowing with Your joy and peace.

Set me on fire to . . .

GOOD MORNING, GOD!
September 26

2 Peter 1:5-8

For this very reason, make every effort to add to your faith goodness; and to goodness, knowledge, and to knowledge, self-control; and to self-control, perseverance, and to perseverance, godliness, and to godliness, brotherly kindness; and to brotherly kindness, love. For, if you possess these qualities in increasing measure, they will keep you from being ineffective and unproductive in your knowledge of our Lord Jesus Christ.

Good Morning, God! O Lord, this is just how I want to be. I want to be so much like Jesus that it can be seen by all. Let me burn with Your Spirit and let me know You so well that I can be an effective witness in all I do. I want to know You more each day and be closer to You. The more I know You the more I love You.

Thank You, Lord Jesus, for . . .

GOOD MORNING, GOD!
September 27

Isaiah 12:4-6

In that day you will say: "Give thanks to the Lord, call on his name; make known among the nations what he has done and proclaim that his name is exalted. Sing to the Lord, for he has done glorious things; let this be known to all the world."

Good Morning, God! Lord, I do *call on Your name.* I know that You are my great Jehovah, my loving protector and provider. Everything I have is from Your hand. You are a great and glorious God of love and mercy. I will exalt Your name in all the earth for You continually fill me with Your Word which brings Your joy and peace.

Send me forth today to . . .

GOOD MORNING, GOD!
September 28

Psalm 111: 1-3

Praise the Lord. I will extol the Lord with all my heart in the council of the upright and in the assembly. Great are the works of the Lord; they are pondered by all who delight in them. Glorious and majestic are his deeds, and his righteousness endures forever.

Good Morning, God! You are a mighty and glorious God. I give You all my thanks and praise. I arise in the morning with songs of praise for You. When I *ponder* all Your glories, I am overwhelmed. You are so good to me. You make my life so precious and sweet. *Great are the works of the Lord; they are pondered by all who delight in them.* I love You, Lord, for Your *righteousness endures forever.*

I will praise You in thanksgiving for . . .

GOOD MORNING, GOD!
September 29

Matthew 26:41

Then he returned to his disciples and found them sleeping. "Could you men not keep watch with me for one hour?" he asked Peter. "Watch and pray so that you will not fall into temptation. The spirit is willing, but the body is weak."

Good Morning, God! I need You to be with me today. I pray that You will guide me and help me to be aware that Satan is doing all he can to lead me astray. I feel so weak but I want to be strong for you. I need to *watch and pray so that I do not fall into temptation.* I need Your power in me to thwart all the arrows of the evil one. I will seek Your council throughout the day and pray that I remain in Your will.

Lead me not into temptation and deliver me from . . .

GOOD MORNING, GOD!
September 30

John 14:12-14

I tell you the truth, anyone who has faith in me will do what I have been doing. He will do even greater things than these, because I am going to the Father. And I will do whatever you ask in my name, so that the Son may bring glory to the Father. You may ask me for anything in my name and I will do it.

Good Morning, God! Precious Jesus, I do have faith in You. I love You and I want to bring glory to You and the Father. Your promises are so wondrous. How can I possibly do greater things than these except with You in my heart. It is hard to conceive that I can ask You for anything and You will do it. You are a mighty and glorious God. Give me the grace to live as You would have me live.

Thank You for loving me so much that . . .

October

GOOD MORNING, GOD!
October 1

2 Corinthians 5:17-18a

Therefore, if anyone is in Christ, he is a new creation; the old has gone the new has come! All this is from God, who reconciled us to himself through Christ and gave us the ministry of reconciliation.

Good Morning, God! What an awesome responsibility You have given me. You have changed me into a *new creation* through the blood of Jesus Christ. I am now Your humble servant. Just as You have reconciled me to You, You call me to reconcile (or bring) others to You. I do so joyfully. Holy Spirit, fill me and give me the words to say, for I know it is not I who speaks but God speaking through me.

Lord, use me to . . .

GOOD MORNING, GOD!
October 2

James 1:16-18

Don't be deceived, my dear brothers. Every good and perfect gift is from above, coming down from the Father of the heavenly lights who does not change like shifting shadows. He chose to give us birth through the word of truth, that we might be a kind of first-fruits of all he created.

Good Morning, God! All that I have is from You – even my life. You have given *every good and perfect gift from above* simply because You love me. Give me the courage to acknowledge this and put my complete trust in You. You will provide all I need and more. You are Eternal and will never leave me. You created me to look to You for everything and when I do, You shower me with Your blessings. Thank You, Lord.

Lord, I will trust You today to . . .

GOOD MORNING, GOD!
October 3

Titus 2:11-14

For the grace of God that brings salvation has appeared to all men, teaching us that, denying ungodliness and worldly lusts, we should live soberly, righteously, and godly in the present age, looking for the blessed hope and glorious appearing of our great God and Savior Jesus Christ, who gave Himself for us, that He might redeem us from every lawless deed and purify for Himself His own special people, zealous for good works.

Good Morning, God! Oh how I long to be able to set aside *all the worldly ungodliness and lusts* that Satan is continually throwing at me. His darts are straight and constant. He knows where my weaknesses are. Help me to know today that You have redeemed us and we are Your *special people.* Help me to lift my shield of faith and stay strong against him.

Jesus, help me to be *zealous for good works* to do Your will and . . .

GOOD MORNING, GOD!
October 4

Ephesians 3:19b-21

. . . and to know this love that surpasses knowledge – that you may be filled to the measure of all the fullness of God. Now to him who is able to do immeasurably more than all we ask or imagine, according to his power that is at work within us, to him be glory in the church and in Christ Jesus throughout all generations, for ever and ever! Amen.

Good Morning, God! How can it be, O Lord; how can it be that You love us so much that we are unable to perceive how great is that love. You love us more than we can imagine – more than our simple minds can comprehend. We can ask anything of You and You hear and answer our prayers. You are with us every minute of the day showering us with Your blessings. You walk with us and guide us even when we don't acknowledge You. Lord, let Your Spirit burn in me today. Set me on fire for You. Let everyone I come near feel the warmth of Your love. I love you, Lord.

Lord, let me bring You glory by . . .

GOOD MORNING, GOD!
October 5

Ephesians 3:16-18

I pray that out of his glorious riches he may strengthen you with power through his Spirit in your inner being, so that Christ may dwell in your hearts through faith. And I pray that you, being rooted and established in love, may have power, together with all the Lord's holy people, to grasp how wide and long and high and deep is the love of Christ.

Good Morning, God! Come into my heart, Lord. Open my heart and mind to the immeasurable power You give us through Your Holy Spirit. Let my faith be so strong and sure that I can feel that power coursing through me and creating a fire within me so I know that I can truly *do all things through Him Who strengthens me.* Remove my fears and anxieties of rejection and send me forth to share Your Good News and love. I want others to know *how wide and long and high and deep is the love of Christ.* Let me show the love of Christ in all I do and say.

Lord, let me claim Your power today to . . .

GOOD MORNING, GOD!
October 6

Psalm 111:9-10

He provided redemption for his people; he ordained his covenant forever —
holy and awesome is his name. The fear of the Lord is the beginning of wisdom; all
who follow his precepts have good understanding. To him belongs eternal praise.

Good Morning, God! Lord, not only do You provide every earthly need
we may have, but You provide even our redemption. You know that we are
sinful by nature and from the foundation of the world You provided Your Son
to be our Savior. You are truly *holy and awesome*. Whom or what shall I fear?
You are my God and Provider. I want to know You more and more so that I
can understand how awesome You are and give You *eternal praise*.

Lord, thank You for . . .

GOOD MORNING, GOD!
October 7

Mark 4:30-32

Again he said, "What shall we say the kingdom of God is like, or what
parable shall we use to describe it? It is like a mustard seed, which is the smallest
seed you plant in the ground. Yet when planted, it grows and becomes the largest
of all garden plants, with such big branches that the birds of the air can perch in
its shade."

Good Morning, God! Father God, let me have faith the size of a mustard
seed. Let Your Word be planted and nurtured in my heart so that my faith
grows and grows. Shower me with Your knowledge and wisdom and let my
faith blossom and expand daily. Let my life be deeply rooted in You. Let my
love for You be a sweet, aromatic gift to You.

Let Your Spirit burn in me and let me grow into . . .

GOOD MORNING, GOD!
October 8

John 17:23-24

I in them and you in me. May they be brought to complete unity to let the world know that you sent me and have loved them even as you have loved me. "Father, I want those you have given me to be with me where I am, and to see my glory, the glory you have given me because you loved me before the creation of the world."

Good Morning, God! How awesome it is that our Lord and Savior prays for us? The King of Glory prays for me and wants me to be where He is. That thought should overshadow anything that I encounter today. The glory of the Lord shines all around me. Let me see that glory and know that You are there for me in everything I do. Let me see that glory and bow before You with all my praise. Show me Your glory and I will fall to my knees in adoration of You.

I am so thankful that You love me, Lord, and . . .

GOOD MORNING, GOD!
October 9

Revelation 22:12-13

"Behold, I am coming soon! My reward is with me, and I will give to everyone according to what he has done. I am the Alpha and the Omega, the First and the Last, the Beginning and the End."

Good Morning, God! Lord, I do believe You are coming soon. I know the world's time and Yours are not the same. However, I know that You say *You will come like a thief in the night.* Help me to be ready. Help me also to do everything possible to be Your witness today. I want everyone I encounter to know that I am Your child and they can be also. Let me feel the urgency to proclaim Your Word so that everyone can know You and love You.

You are the *Beginning and the End.* Let my life be such that . . .

GOOD MORNING, GOD!
October 10

Isaiah 41:9-10

I took you from the ends of the earth; from its farthest corners I called you. I said, "You are my servant; I have chosen you and have not rejected you. So do not fear, for I am with you; do not be dismayed for I am your God. I will strengthen you and help you; I will uphold you with my righteous right hand."

Good Morning, God! What an incredible Word from You. What more could I ask: *You have called me. I am Your servant; You will strengthen me and help me with your own righteous right hand.* This is so powerful. It is not about what I can do but what **You** can do through me. You have called me to be Your servant and You will give me everything I need to accomplish the task before me. Praise God! Praise God!

Lord, thank You for the power of Your Word and help me to . . .

GOOD MORNING, GOD!
October 11

Psalm 40:4-5

Blessed is the man who makes the Lord his trust, who does not look to the proud, to those who turn aside to false gods. Many, O Lord my God, are the wonders you have done. The things you planned for us no one can recount to you; were I to speak and tell of them, they would be too many to declare.

Good Morning, God! Oh how wonderful it is to think of all the bountiful things You have done for me. You shower me with more blessings than I can count each day. You are always there and ready to give me more than I could ever expect or desire. You are a God of goodness and blessing. You delight in letting Your blessings rain over me to the point of overflowing. I am so incredibly blessed. Thank You, Lord.

Let me share my blessings by . . .

GOOD MORNING, GOD!
October 12

Luke 21:29-33

He told them this parable: "Look at the fig tree and all the trees. When they sprout leaves, you can see for yourselves and know that summer is near. Even so, when you see these things happening, you know that the kingdom of God is near. I tell you the truth this generation will certainly not pass away until all these things have happened. Heaven and earth will pass away, but my words will never pass away."

Good Morning, God! Lord, this has always been a hard scripture for me to understand. You are talking to Your disciples and they surely will pass away before Your Kingdom shall come. I think You are telling us that the Kingdom is near and the "generation" of your chosen people will not pass away until all these things have happened. Lord, I know Your Word is our rock and salvation. It will never pass away. We can rely on it to sustain us throughout any tribulation. Thank You, Lord.

Lord, help me to further Your Kingdom by . . .

GOOD MORNING, GOD!
October 13

John 3:35-36

For the one whom God has sent speaks the words of God, for God gives the Spirit without limit. The Father loves the Son and has placed everything in his hands. Whoever believes in the Son has eternal life, but whoever rejects the Son will not see life, for God's wrath remains on him.

Good Morning, God! *The Spirit without limit* – Oh, Lord, that is immeasurable power. You love the Son and *have placed everything in his hands.* Through Him, I also have the power of the Holy Spirit and *eternal life.* How can I not use that Power to share the Gospel and tell everyone the Good News? Lord, don't let it be on my hands that one of Your children should perish because I did not witness of Your love and mercy.

Give me the Words to speak today to . . .

GOOD MORNING, GOD!
October 14

Romans 14:10-12

You, then, why do you judge your brother? Or why do you look down on your brother? For we will all stand before God's judgment seat. It is written: "As surely as I live, says the Lord, every knee will bow before me; every tongue will confess to God."

Good Morning, God! Lord, You know this is one of my greatest sins. I am so ready to judge everyone. I think it is the Pharisee coming out in me. I don't truly think I am holier than thou, but sometimes it is really hard not to condemn others for their actions or lack thereof. Help me to know that You are the only judge of mankind. You alone are God, and You alone can judge the hearts of others. Help me to be filled with Your mercy – the mercy You show me every day.

Lord, let me see the goodness in others so that I can . . .

GOOD MORNING, GOD!
October 15

Revelation 22:3b-5

The throne of God and of the Lamb will be in the city, and his servants will serve him. They will see his face, and his name will be on their foreheads. There will be no more night. They will not need the light of a lamp or the light of the sun, for the Lord God will give them light. And they will reign for ever and ever.

Good Morning, God! Come, Lord Jesus, come! This is the story of Your glory and Your kingdom. What a glorious day! I want to *see Your face.* I want to be so close to You. We will be with You and Your light will overpower any other light we have ever known. The Son will be brighter than the sun! This will be Your day of glory. Your Kingdom will *reign for ever and ever.* Praise God!

Lord, I look forward to serving You by . . .

GOOD MORNING, GOD!
October 16

James 3: 9-11

With the tongue we praise our Lord and Father, and with it we curse men, who have been made in God's likeness. Out of the same mouth come praise and cursing. My brothers this should not be. Can both fresh water and salt water flow from the same spring?

Good Morning, God! Oh, Lord. I can't tell You how many times I wish I could have bitten off my tongue. I let the evil one consume me and let his words come forth instead of Yours. I am so sorry when this happens. I feel so evil and far away from You. Let me use my words to only bring You praise and glory. Don't let my words spew out venom from Satan. I only want to praise You with every word from my mouth.

Lord, let my words only be Your Words of encouragement to . . .

GOOD MORNING, GOD!
October 17

Daniel 3: 24-25

Then King Nebuchadnezzar leaped to his feet in amazement and asked his advisors, "Weren't there three men that we tied and up and threw into the fire?" They replied, "Certainly, O king." He said, "Look! I see four men walking around in the fire, unbound and unharmed, and the fourth looks like a son of the gods."

Good Morning, God! How can I go about with so little faith? When things start to get the slightest bit "warm" I start worrying and begin to panic. I've heard the story of Shadrach, Meshach and Abednego since I was a child in Sunday School. I remember the flannel-graph figures on the board. It was so easy to believe then. Why do I now doubt Your faithfulness. Increase my faith, Oh God! Help me remember You are with me *until the end of the age.*

Lord, give me a stronger faith to . . .

GOOD MORNING, GOD!
October 18

Esther 4:14

"For if you remain silent at this time, relief and deliverance for the Jews will arise from another place, but you and your father's family will perish. And who knows but that you have come to royal position for such a time as this?"

Good Morning, God! First of all, Dear God, let me know that deliverance will come. You promise deliverance in the gift of Your Son who died for my sins. But, let me know that because of His sacrifice, I also have a job to do to bring about the redemption of others. You have placed me in this particular place at this particular time to bring about Your salvation to others. Give me Your words to speak that they may hear what it is You have to say!

Lord, don't let me remain silent because . . .

GOOD MORNING, GOD!
October 19

Isaiah 40:30-31

Even youths grow tired and weary, and young men stumble and fall; but those who hope in the Lord will renew their strength. They will soar on wings like eagles; they will run and not grow weary, they will walk and not be faint.

Good Morning, God! This scripture has never meant so much to me as it does now that I am aging. When I was young I never considered *growing weary*. I was invincible. Now, Oh Lord, I realize how much I need You. I need Your renewed strength because I have a mission to complete for You. Give me the strength that only faith can give – strength to endure no matter what the odds because I have the power of Your Holy Spirit. I love the idea of *soaring on wings like eagles* – such freedom and peace.

I feel renewed because I know Your Spirit will give me the power to . . .

GOOD MORNING, GOD!
October 20

Romans 5:20-21

The law was added so that the trespass might increase. But where sin increased, grace increased all the more, so that, just as sin reigned in death, so also grace might reign through righteousness to bring eternal life through Jesus Christ our Lord.

Good Morning, God! Oh, God! How great is Your grace. No matter how many sins I commit, Your grace is sufficient to cover them all! I don't deserve it. I am guilty. I sin when I don't want to. I know better and I hate myself for it. But, that is the glory of Your grace. Your *grace increases all the more.* Your grace is unmerited forgiveness and love. I can never out-sin Your grace. You are our Perfect Loving Father! Praise God from Whom all blessings flow!

Thank You, Lord. Thank You for Your grace and . . .

GOOD MORNING, GOD!
October 21

Ephesians 1:17-18

I keep asking that the God of our Lord Jesus Christ, the glorious Father may give you the Spirit of wisdom and revelation so that you may know him better. I pray also that the eyes of your heart may be enlightened in order that you may know the hope to which he has called you, the riches of your glorious inheritance in the saints.

Good Morning, God! Oh God! Help me to take this scripture into my heart. Let it completely consume me. Let me know You as *the glorious Father.* Let me be like Paul and truly know who You are and how awesome and wonderful You are. Let Your Spirit open *the eyes of my heart* so that I can realize how awesome it is to be a child of God and have the glorious inheritance to spend eternity with you. Can I truly be one of Your saints? By the grace of God, yes, I can! Thank you, Lord Jesus.

Lord, *I keep asking You* to . . .

GOOD MORNING, GOD!
October 22

Philemon 1:4-7

I always thank my God as I remember you in my prayers, because I hear about your faith in the Lord Jesus and your love for all the saints. I pray that you may be active in sharing your faith, so that you will have a full understanding of every good thing we have in Christ. Your love has given me great joy and encouragement, because you, brother, have refreshed the hearts of the saints.

Good Morning, God! I only hope that You can remember me *because of my faith in the Lord Jesus and my love for all the saints.* I pray that I can continually be active in sharing my faith. I want everyone to know the glory it is to be Your child. All good things come from You. Give me the words to share this great truth with others. Let them know the joy it is to be blessed by You.

I always thank my God for . . .

GOOD MORNING, GOD!
October 23

John 15:15-17

I no longer call you servants, because a servant does not know his master's business. Instead, I have called you friends, for everything that I learned from my Father I have made known to you. You did not choose me, but I chose you and appointed you to go and bear fruit – fruit that will last. Then the Father will give you whatever you ask in my name. This is my command: Love each other.

Good Morning, God! I am filled with wonder at the thought of being called Your friend and that I am chosen by You. I know it is true, but it is so hard to comprehend. I am so thankful that You have chosen me to *bear fruit that will last.* My joy in life is sharing Your Word and loving Your children. My greatest desire is to further Your Kingdom and let everyone know the joy it is to be Your child.

I love you, Friend Jesus. Help me to . . .

GOOD MORNING, GOD!
October 24

Daniel 3:26b-27

Then Shadrach, Meshach and Abednego came out of the fire, and the satraps, prefects, governors and royal advisers crowded around them. They saw that the fire had not harmed their bodies, nor was a hair of their heads singed; their robes were not scorched and there was no smell of fire on them.

Good Morning, God! O what an awesome God we serve! You are mighty to save. You are all powerful and forever watching over Your children. Lord, help me to remember that no matter what Satan may attempt, his fate is sealed. You reign and are in control. Satan will be thrown into the fiery pit and I will reign with You in heaven forever and ever. Praise God!

Lord, when I feel the fires around me, help me to . . .

GOOD MORNING, GOD!
October 25

Psalm 102:1-2

Hear my prayer, O Lord; let my cry for help come to you. Do not hide your face from me when I am in distress. Turn your ear to me; when I call, answer me quickly.

Good Morning, God! Sometimes I feel so far away from You, O Lord. I feel as if my prayers are empty and never reach the ceiling much less heaven. Lord, I know You have not moved and when I feel this way it is because I am the one who has left Your side. I hate to feel this way. I need you to *answer me quickly* for I am in despair. Let me feel Your arms around me, holding me in Your bosom.

Keep me close, Dear Savior. Let me know You are by my side so I can . . .

GOOD MORNING, GOD!
October 26

Proverbs 27:17-18

As iron sharpens iron, so one man sharpens another. He who tends a fig tree will eat its fruit and he who looks after his master will be honored.

Good Morning, God! Lord, I know my purpose in life is to bring You glory in all I do. I thank You for the people with whom You have surrounded me who encourage and share in my journey. It is an awesome journey. I am closer and closer to You each day. I want to do Your work and bring others closer to You also. I know You are my *Master* and I want to honor You in all I do.

Thank You for my Christian friends who . . .

GOOD MORNING, GOD!
October 27

Ephesians 1:3-4a

Praise be to the God and Father of our Lord Jesus Christ, who has blessed us in the heavenly realms with every spiritual blessing in Christ. For he chose us in him before the creation of the world to be holy and blameless in his sight.

Good Morning, God! Praise be to You, O Lord. You continually shower me with Your blessings. My cup overflows. Your mercy and grace consume me. When I think of what a terrible sinner I am, it grieves me and I know it grieves You as well. *You chose me before the creation of the world* to be Your child. The only way I can be *holy and blameless in Your sight* is through Your grace. Thank You, Lord, for loving me and forgiving me.

Let me praise You today by . . .

GOOD MORNING, GOD!
October 28

Hebrews 4:14-15

Therefore, since we have a great high priest who has gone through the heavens, Jesus the Son of God, let us hold firmly to the faith we profess. For we do not have a high priest who is unable to sympathize with our weaknesses, but we have one who has been tempted in every way, just as we are – yet was without sin.

Good Morning, God! Lord, You know my every thought and every weakness. You know my desire to be the person You created me to be and You know how I fall short. I give You thanks and praise that You can *sympathize* with me for You have encountered far more than I could ever face. You were tempted and yet You did not fail but stood fast against the devil. Give me the strength and courage to do the same.

Fill me with Your Spirit to overcome . . .

GOOD MORNING, GOD!
October 29

1 John 8-10

If we claim to be without sin, we deceive ourselves and the truth is not in us. If we confess our sins, he is faithful and just and will forgive us our sins and purify us from all unrighteousness. If we claim we have not sinned, we make him out to be a liar and his word has no place in our lives.

Good Morning, God! Precious Savior, I know I am a sinner. Many times, I sin before I even get out of bed in the morning. My evil thoughts get the best of me. I try so hard not to let my sins overcome me but I continually fall short. I do *confess my sins* – even the sins of omission of which I am so guilty. Please *forgive my sins and purify me from all unrighteousness.* I don't want to sin. I want to be washed in the blood of Jesus.

As a forgiven child of God, help me to . . .

GOOD MORNING, GOD!
October 30

Philippians 4:8-9

    Finally, brothers, whatever is true, whatever is noble, whatever is right, whatever is pure, whatever is lovely, whatever is admirable – if anything is excellent or praiseworthy – think about such things. Whatever you have learned or received or heard from me, or seen in me – put it into practice. And the God of peace will be with you.

    Good Morning, God! Lord, why do I let this world get me down? Why do I complain and feel sorry for myself? Why do I delight in my very own little pity party? There is so much to be thankful for. I could go on and on thanking You for all the lovely things You have given me. Let me dwell on those things and not the bad. Fill my heart with Your joy and peace. Let me *learn, receive and hear from You and put it into practice.*

    Thank You, Jesus. Let me especially thank You for . . .

GOOD MORNING, GOD!
October 31

Proverbs 3:7-9

    Do not be wise in your own eyes; fear the Lord and shun evil. This will bring health to your body and nourishment to your bones. Honor the Lord with your wealth, with the first fruits of all your crops; then your barns will be filled to overflowing, and your vats will brim over with new wine.

    Good Morning, God! Not for one minute do I think *I am wise in my own eyes.* I know how foolish I am and the foolish things I do. But, I do *honor You with my first fruits.* Tithing has made such a difference in my life. I feel Your blessings *which are overflowing.* You promise blessings to those who tithe. It hurts me to think of the blessings people are missing by not obeying Your command to do so.

    Thank You for Your rich blessings and help me to . . .

✠ ✠ ✠

November

GOOD MORNING, GOD!
November 1

Romans 8:28-29

And we know that in all things God works for the good of those who love him, who have been called according to his purpose. For those God foreknew he also predestined to be conformed to the likeness of his Son that he might be the firstborn among many brothers.

Good Morning, God! What glorious Words to start my day. Even though it may seem that I am on the brink of destruction, You make *all things work for the good.* It never seems possible when disaster strikes that it can be turned to good, but I have seen You work through these things many times in my life. I am Your blessed child – *the firstborn among many brothers.* I have the inheritance of the King. All is good!

Lord, help to always remember . . .

GOOD MORNING, GOD!
November 2

1 Corinthians 10:12-13

So, if you think you are standing firm, be careful that you don't fall! No temptation has seized you except what is common to man. And God is faithful; he will not let you be tempted beyond what you can bear. But when you are tempted, he will also provide a way out so that you can stand up under it.

Good Morning, God! What a glorious promise, O God! Even when I feel I am walking through the valley of trials and tribulations; even when Satan's flaming arrows are falling all around me, You will not let me fall. You suffered and were tempted so much more than I can ever be and yet You love me so much that You will *provide a way out so I can stand up under it.* Thank You, Jesus.

When I am seized by temptation, help me to . . .

GOOD MORNING, GOD!
November 3

Ephesians 1:4b-8

In love he predestined us to be adopted as his sons through Jesus Christ, in accordance with his pleasure and will — to the praise of his glorious grace, which he has freely given us in the One he loves. In him we have redemption through his blood, the forgiveness of sins, in accordance with the riches of God's grace that he lavished on us with all wisdom and understanding.

Good Morning, God! I love to think that I have been *predestined to be adopted as Your son through Jesus Christ.* I'm not predestined to the point that I don't have free will but because of Your love and grace, You have chosen me to be Your child. I am *redeemed through the blood and forgiven through Your grace.* You lavish me with Your blessings. My heart overflows with love and thanksgiving for You.

Thank You for loving me, Lord, and . . .

GOOD MORNING, GOD!
November 4

Hebrews 10:15-17

The Holy Spirit also testifies to us about this. For he says: "This is the covenant I will make with them after that time, says the Lord. I will put my laws in their hearts, and will write them on their minds." Then he adds: "Their sins and lawless acts I will remember no more."

Good Morning, God! Precious Holy Spirit, pray for me. Let my heart be filled with the Fire of Your love and keep me ever close to You. Teach me Your ways and keep them in my heart and mind. I am so thankful that my life is a part of Your Covenant. Thank You for *remembering my sins no more.* I am forgiven. I am free. Praise God!

Lord, I give You praise for . . .

GOOD MORNING, GOD!
November 5

1 John 2:4-6

The man who says, "I know him," but does not do what he commands is a liar, and the truth is not in him. But if any one obeys his word, God's love is truly made complete in him. This is how we know we are in him: Whoever claims to live in him must walk as Jesus did.

Good Morning, God! Help me to *walk as Jesus did.* Let me be *truly made complete in Him.* Help me to be obedient. I want to know You better and love You more. Use me to be Your light shining on the path to guide others to You. Let me live so that others can see You through me. Use me, Lord. *Here am I, send me.*

Lord, use me to . . .

GOOD MORNING, GOD!
November 6

2 Thessalonians 2:13-14

But we ought always to thank God for you, brothers loved by the Lord, because from the beginning God chose you to be saved through the sanctifying work of the Spirit and through belief in the truth. He called you to this through our gospel that you might share in the glory of Our Lord Jesus Christ.

Good Morning, God! I am *loved by the Lord.* How awesome is that to hear as I start my day! Thank You, Lord, for choosing me. Thank You for the gift of Your Son and Your sanctifying grace by which I am saved *that I might share in the glory of Our Lord Jesus Christ.* I am filled with Your love and my heart is singing. Praise God from Whom all blessings flow. You are an awesome God!

Let these Words ring in my ears all day and help me to . . .

GOOD MORNING, GOD!
November 7

1 Corinthians 12:27-28

Now you are the body of Christ, and each one of you is a part of it. And in the church God has appointed first of all apostles, second prophets, third teachers, then workers of miracles, also those having the gifts of healing, those able to help others, those with gifts of administration and those speaking in different kinds of tongues.

Good Morning, God! Lord, I know You have given each of us the gifts we need to do the tasks You have assigned to us. Your Word proclaims this fact and I believe it with all my heart. Help me to know what Your purpose is for me. For I know I've been called as part of the *body of Christ* and I know You will provide the gifts needed to accomplish all You have planned for me.

Thank You for using me to . . .

GOOD MORNING, GOD!
November 8

2 Corinthians 9:11-12

You will be made rich in every way so that you can be generous on every occasion, and through us your generosity will result in thanksgiving to God. This service that you perform is not only supplying the needs of God's people but is also overflowing in many expressions of thanks to God.

Good Morning, God! Lord, I am so richly blessed. I am filled with love and thanksgiving to You for Your lavish blessings to me. I am rich far beyond all my expectations. I know I don't deserve this, but You are a God of grace. How can I not *be generous and* share with others from the abundance You have given me? I want to return Your goodness to Your people.

Help me to *express my thanks to You* by. . .

GOOD MORNING, GOD!
November 9

Galatians 3:26-28

You are all sons of God through faith in Christ Jesus, for all of you who were baptized into Christ have clothed yourselves with Christ. There is neither Jew nor Greek, slave nor free, male nor female, for you are all one in Christ Jesus.

Good Morning, God! I love the thought of being *clothed with Christ.* I love the idea of having Him wrapped around me and filling me with His love and mercy. I long to feel the softness of His touch and the warmth of His arms encircling me. Fill me with Your love for others. Let me love as You do, for then I will be *one in Christ Jesus.*

Lord, increase my faith so that . . . .

GOOD MORNING, GOD!
November 10

Colossians 3:15-17

Let the peace of Christ rule in your hearts, since as members of one body you were called to peace. And be thankful. Let the word of Christ dwell in you richly as you teach and admonish one another with all wisdom, and as you sing psalms, hymns and spiritual songs with gratitude in your hearts to God. And whatever you do, whether in word or deed, do it all in the name of the Lord Jesus, giving thanks to God the Father through him.

Good Morning, God! Oh how I long to have *the peace of Christ rule in my heart.* Your Peace is one of Your greatest gifts. Without the Peace of Christ, I have nothing. Don't let Satan steal that Peace away. Let Your Word dwell in me. I am so thankful and want to share that Peace with everyone I meet. I give You thanks and praise, Father God, for You are good. Your mercies overwhelm me.

Let everything I do today be . . .

GOOD MORNING, GOD!
November 11

Deuteronomy 6: 4-7

Hear, O Israel: The Lord our God, the Lord is one. Love the Lord your God with all your heart and with all your soul and with all your strength. These commandments that I give you today are to be upon your hearts. Impress them on your children. Talk about them when you sit at home and when you walk along the road, when you lie down and when you get up.

Good Morning, God! O Lord, I do love You. I try to love You with *all my heart and soul and strength.* When I consider all Your wonders and blessings, I can only love You more. Lord, help me to *impress this on my children.* Help me to show them the glory of Who You are and Your goodness. Let it be my life's mission to tell my children about You. Let them grow up as a child of God, filled with all Your blessings, grace and mercy.

I want to talk about You today when . . .

GOOD MORNING, GOD!
November 12

Psalm 105:1-4

Give thanks to the Lord, call on his name; make known among the nations what he has done. Sing to him, sing praise to him; tell of all his wonderful acts. Glory in his holy name; let the hearts of those who seek the Lord rejoice. Look to the Lord and his strength; seek his face always. . ."

Good Morning, God! Oh how wonderful it is to *be able to call on Your name.* I truly *sing praise to You.* I want to *tell of all Your wonderful acts.* I am truly a child of God and I *seek Your face always.* I *look to You for my strength.* Use me, Lord, to *make it known among the nations what You have done.* I will *rejoice* in You always. You are my joy and my peace. Thank You, Lord.

All praise and glory to You O Lord . . .

GOOD MORNING, GOD!
November 13

Luke 3:15-16

The people were waiting expectantly and were all wondering in their hearts if John might possibly be the Christ. John answered them all, "I baptize you with water. But one more powerful than I will come, the thongs of whose sandals I am not worthy to untie. He will baptize you with the Holy Spirit and with fire. . ."

Good Morning, God! Lord, baptize me with Your Spirit. Set me on fire for You. Set my feet on the path of Your righteousness. I know I am not worthy, Lord, but I know that You can use me. You fill me with Your Spirit and send me forth. Let my words be Your Words and my thoughts be Your thoughts. Let Your light shine through me. Let me declare the Word of God to all I encounter. Let them be filled with Your joy.

I am *not worthy to untie Your sandals,* but use me to . . .

GOOD MORNING, GOD!
November 14

Jeremiah 9:23-24

This is what the Lord says: "Let not the wise boast of their wisdom or the strong boast of their strength or the rich boast of their riches, but let the one who boasts boast about this: that they have the understanding to know me, that I am the Lord, who exercises kindness, justice and righteousness on earth, for in these I delight," declares the Lord.

Good Morning, God! Lord, I am so thankful that You have chosen me to be Your child. What joy it is to know that I am a child of the Most High God and an heir to the riches of Your salvation. Make me to be humble, Lord. Help me to understand what a privilege it is to be able to boast of our loving relationship. Help me to *exercise kindness, justice and righteousness on earth.*

I want to bring You glory and honor in all I do. Help me to . . .

GOOD MORNING, GOD!
November 15

Psalm 127:1-2

Unless the Lord builds the house, the builders labor in vain. Unless the Lord watches over the city, the guards stand watch in vain. In vain you rise early and stay up late, toiling for food to eat — for he grants sleep to those he loves.

Good Morning, God! Lord, help me to *be still and know that You are God.* Why do I feel it is up to me to calm the raging waves around me? I know from Your Word that You alone are the sovereign Master of the universe. You have the power and might to bring about calm and peace no matter what is going on around me. Help me not to *labor in vain* when all I have to do is call on Your Name and You will be by my side. I know You love me so why do I worry?

Lord, let me feel Your calmness surrounding me and . . .

GOOD MORNING, GOD!
November 16

Hebrews 12:10-11

Our fathers disciplined us for a little while as they thought best; but God disciplines us for our good, that we may share in his holiness. No discipline seems pleasant at the time, but painful. Later on, however, it produces a harvest of righteousness and peace for those who have been trained by it.

Good Morning, God! You know that lack of discipline is one of my worst faults. I start each day with the best laid plans and intentions, but by the end of the day, I am lacking. I thank You that You gently discipline me with Your loving heart and hands. I need You to guide me and show me the path to Your righteousness and peace. It is through Your love and grace that I am an heir to Your eternity. Thank You, Lord.

Father, guide me today to . . .

GOOD MORNING, GOD!
November 17

Psalm 121:5-8

The Lord watches over you—the Lord is your shade at your right hand; the sun will not harm you by day, nor the moon by night. The Lord will keep you from all harm—he will watch over your coming and going both now and forevermore.

Good Morning, God! O Lord, how wonderful it is to know that You are watching over me and protecting me. *You will not let the sun harm me by day, nor the moon by night.* That pretty much covers any situation I may find myself. It is hard for me to comprehend how much You love me and how omniscient You are. You know everything about me and still love me. Since You *watch over my coming and going* I have nothing to fear. You will be right there with me every step of my life – guiding and keeping me from harm.

I give thanks to You, O Lord, for . . .

GOOD MORNING, GOD!
November 18

Deuteronomy 20:3-4

He shall say: "Hear, O Israel, today you are going into battle against your enemies. Do not be fainthearted or afraid; do not be terrified or give way to panic before them. For the Lord your God is the one who goes with you to fight for you against your enemies to give you victory."

Good Morning, God! It seems that some days are nothing but an uphill battle. There are so many things pulling me this way and that. I am so thankful that in the midst of my enemies, whether real or metaphorical, You are with me. You are bigger than any problem that I could have. Don't let me *be fainthearted or afraid; don't let me be terrified or give way to panic before them.* You are greater than any care that burdens my heart. You are an awesome God of love and mercy.

Lord, give me victory over . . .

GOOD MORNING, GOD!
November 19

1 John 3:1-2

How great is the love the Father has lavished on us, that we should be called children of God! And that is what we are! The reason the world does not know us is that it did not know him. Dear friends, now we are children of God, and what we will be has not yet been made known. But we know that when he appears, we shall be like him, for we shall see him as he is.

Good Morning, God! I am a child of God! I am a child of God! I want to say it again and again. How wonderful it is to know that I am a child of God and *what I will be has not yet been made known.* Father, You love us so dearly that You *lavish* Your love upon us. I see You and Your glory all around me. The wonder of Your love is amazing. I feel Your arms around me pulling me closer and closer to You. Let me *be like You.*

Thank You, God, for . . .

GOOD MORNING, GOD!
November 20

Colossians 3:1-4

Since, then, you have been raised with Christ, set your hearts on things above, where Christ is seated at the right hand of God. Set your minds on things above, not on earthly things. For you died, and your life is now hidden with Christ in God. When Christ, who is your life, appears, then you also will appear with him in glory.

Good Morning, God! Help me today to keep my perspective completely toward You and You alone. Let me realize that the things of this world are only temporary and not worth the energy I spend worrying about them. Let me know that You reign and Your will is done. All that matters is You and that I have given myself to you. I can't wait to *appear with him in glory!* Praise God!

Since I have been raised with Christ, help me to . . .

GOOD MORNING, GOD!
November 21

John 16:13-15

But when he, the Spirit of truth, comes, he will guide you into all truth. He will not speak on his own; he will speak only what he hears, and he will tell you what is yet to come. He will bring glory to me by taking from what is mine and making it known to you. All that belongs to the Father is mine. That is why I said the Spirit will take from what is mine and make it known to you.

Good Morning, God! Holy Spirit, pray for me. Pray that I might open my heart and mind to know the mind of Christ. Let me be more and more like Jesus each day. Lord, thank You for the gift of Your Spirit to enlighten me and let me know You better and love You more. Let me hear what it is You are saying to me today and let everything I do bring You glory.

I love You, Lord, and . . .

GOOD MORNING, GOD!
November 22

Daniel 3:17-18

If we are thrown into the blazing furnace, the God we serve is able to save us from it, and he will rescue us from your hand, O king. But even if he does not, we want you to know, O king that we will not serve your gods or worship the image of gold you have set up.

Good Morning, God! Oh God, what faith is this that can stand in the face of death and know that You alone are our strength and Redeemer. You will deliver us from the *blazing furnaces* we face each day. I want to have faith so strong that I will not fear anything the world has for me. I serve the Most High God and will not be swayed. I will not worship the *image of gold* that seems so enticing. I worship You alone.

Lord, I worship You with . . .

GOOD MORNING, GOD!
November 23

Psalm 24:8-10

Who is the King of glory? The Lord strong and mighty, the Lord mighty in battle. Lift up your heads, you gates; lift them up, you ancient doors, that the King of glory may come in. Who is he, this King of glory? The Lord Almighty – he is the King of glory.

Good Morning, God! Lord, it is so hard for me to imagine You in Your Glory. You have created us to bring You glory. I now understand why. If we could see You in Your Glory we would completely understand who You are and would worship You with our whole heart. We would fall as if dead as John did in The Revelation. Your Glory would consume us and we would worship You continually.

Lord, show me Your Glory and let me . . .

GOOD MORNING, GOD!
November 24

1 Chronicles 16:8-10

Give thanks to the Lord, call on his name; make known among the nations what he has done. Sing to him, sing praise to him; tell of all his wonderful acts. Glory in his holy name; let the hearts of those who seek the Lord rejoice.

Good Morning, God! Lord, You know I call on You every day and many times a day. I am so thankful to know that I can call on You, my God and my King, and know that You are right there to help me with whatever I need. I would be engulfed with the despicable things of this world, if not for You. It is such a comfort to know You will always be there.

I *sing praises to You for Your wonderful acts.* I want everyone to know *all that You have done.* Let me praise You today by . . .

GOOD MORNING, GOD!
November 25

Psalm 95:1-3

Come, let us sing for joy to the Lord; let us shout aloud to the Rock of our salvation. Let us come before him with thanksgiving and extol him with music and song. For the Lord is the great God, the great King above all gods.

Good Morning, God! In this season of Thanksgiving, my first thoughts turn to You. You alone are the *Rock of our salvation.* You give this country a solid foundation upon which to stand. You have blessed us so incredibly. I *come before you with thanksgiving.* All our blessings are from You alone. You have blessed this land and we know that as long as we remain *One Nation Under God* You will continue to shower us with Your blessings.

I sing praises to You, our *great God, the great King above all gods.* Let me show my praise by . . .

GOOD MORNING, GOD!
November 26

Psalm 98:1-2

Sing to the Lord a new song, for he has done marvelous things; his right hand and his holy arm have worked salvation for him. The Lord has made his salvation known and revealed his righteousness to the nations.

Good Morning, God! Lord, I rise up singing and praising Your Holy Name. You have filled my heart with joy and peace – *the peace of Christ that passes all understanding.* I feel so unworthy, but I understand that Grace is who You are. You have offered us salvation and *revealed your righteousness to the nations.* Oh that we would keep that in the forefront of our hearts – that You are our Lord and Savior. We are saved by Your grace alone.

Thank You, Father, for Your blessings and grace and . . .

GOOD MORNING, GOD!
November 27

Psalm 100:1-5

Shout for joy to the Lord, all the earth. Worship the Lord with gladness; come before him with joyful songs. Know that the Lord is God. It is he who made us, and we are his; we are his people, the sheep of his pasture. Enter his gates with thanksgiving and his courts with praise; give thanks to him and praise his name. For the Lord is good and his love endures forever; his faithfulness continues through all generations.

Good Morning, God! Lord, help me to remember today that You are God and I'm not. Help me to remember that I am merely a *sheep in Your pasture* and I don't have to be in control. I will *enter Your gates with thanksgiving and Your courts with praise.* You created us and You will continue to love us and bless us. *For the Lord is good and his love endures forever; Your faithfulness continues through all generations.*

Lord, I *worship You with gladness* and . . .

GOOD MORNING, GOD!
November 28

1 Timothy 4:8-10

For physical training is of some value, but godliness has value for all things, holding promise for both the present life and the life to come. This is a trustworthy saying that deserves full acceptance (and for this we labor and strive), that we have put our hope in the living God, who is the Savior of all men, and especially of those who believe.

Good Morning, God! Lord, all our hope is in You. You have blessed us much more than we could ever dream. Teach me to be godly in all things. Let me cling to the promise that You are *the Savior of all men, and especially for those who believe.* Increase my faith to hold on to that promise. Let me strive for a life that is pleasing to You and will be a beacon for others to know You.

Lord, I give thanks for . . .

GOOD MORNING, GOD!
November 29

Revelation 4:10-11

The twenty-four elders fall down before him who sits on the throne, and worship him who lives for ever and ever. They lay their crowns before the throne and say: "You are worthy, our Lord and God, to receive glory and honor and power, for you created all things, and by your will they were created and have their being."

Good Morning, God! What a beautiful picture of heaven – pure worship and *glory and honor.* Lord, we have so much to be thankful for. You died that we might one day spend eternity with You. I give You thanks and praise for all Your goodness, mercy and grace. I want to lay *my crown before You and say You alone are worthy.*

Lord, thank You for blessing me beyond my imagination and help me to . . .

GOOD MORNING, GOD!
November 30

Deuteronomy 7:18-19

But do not be afraid of them; remember well what the Lord your God did to Pharaoh and to all Egypt. You saw with your own eyes the great trials, the miraculous signs and wonders, the mighty hand and outstretched arm, with which the Lord your God brought you out. The Lord your God will do the same to all the peoples you now fear.

Good Morning, God! Oh, what a mighty and powerful God You are. How can I let myself fall into despair when I see all the wonders You have done? I see Your miracles around me at every turn and yet I fear things over which I have no control. I know *You will bring me out.* Lord, help me to remember that we are Your children and You will defeat any foe we may have, either physical or of our own contriving.

Lord, let me be at peace today knowing You are in control and . . .

December

GOOD MORNING, GOD!
December 1

Isaiah 42:6-7

I, the Lord, have called you in righteousness; I will keep you and will make you to be a covenant for the people and a light for the Gentiles, to open eyes that are blind, to free captives from prison and to release from the dungeon those who sit in darkness.

Good Morning, God! It is difficult for me to conceive that You are calling me to be a light to Your people. I feel so inadequate, but *You have called me in righteousness*. If You are calling me, what can I do but say, "yes." Let me feel the power of Your Holy Spirit within me and send me forth with Your message. You tell us *not to worry about what we will say*. I know You will be right by my side every step of the way.

Lord, guide me to be Your . . .

GOOD MORNING, GOD!
December 2

Matthew 6:25-26

"Therefore I tell you, do not worry about your life, what you will eat or drink; or about your body, what you will wear. Is not life more than food, and the body more than clothes. Look at the birds of the air; they do not sow or reap or store away in barns, and yet your heavenly Father feeds them. Are you not much more valuable than they?"

Good Morning, God! Oh, Lord, why do I worry? Your Word is completely clear on the fact that You will provide all that I need. Why do I let myself get so caught up in thinking that it is all up to me? I know You love me so much that You gave Your only Son to die for me. What more could I ask or need? I love you, Lord.

Help me to keep You close by today and . . .

GOOD MORNING, GOD!
December 3

Galatians 2:20-21

I have been crucified with Christ and I no longer live, but Christ lives in me. The life I now live in the body, I live by faith in the Son of God, who loved me and gave himself for me. I do not set aside the grace of God, for if righteousness could be gained through the law, Christ died for nothing!

Good Morning, God! The most glorious gift that could ever be given is *Christ lives in me!* What great wonders that evokes. *Christ lives in me!* When I think about it I am overwhelmed with the idea of the possibility of me becoming more like Christ. I have His love, power, grace, compassion and every aspect of His perfect being right at my access, if I only acknowledge that He lives in me. Thank You, Lord.

Lord, help me to use Your power today to . . .

GOOD MORNING, GOD!
December 4

Romans 15:13

May the God of hope fill you with all joy and peace as you trust in him, so that you may overflow with hope by the power of the Holy Spirit?

Good Morning, God! *Hope* is a beautiful word. Without hope we are lost and destitute. We lose our purpose and our joy. We are in the abyss and can't see any way out. But, because of Your great love for us, You have given us Your Holy Spirit. Through Your Holy Spirit we can do all things. We are *filled with all joy and peace.* I do trust You, Lord. My heart is overflowing with the joy of Your hope within me. Thank you, Precious Savior.

Show me how to share that hope with . . .

GOOD MORNING, GOD!
December 5

John 14:26-27

But the Advocated, the Holy Spirit, whom the Father will send in my name, will teach you all things and will remind you of everything I have said to you. Peace I leave with you; my peace I give to you. I do not give to you as the world gives. Do not let your hearts be troubled and do not be afraid.

Good Morning, God! Sweet Jesus, I can feel your arms around me as I read these words. Nothing is more comforting than knowing that I will be engulfed in Your peace. No matter how desolate things may seem, You are Peace and You are comforting me. The only true peace comes from You. Men may think they can create their own peace through their own works, but it is futile without Your blessing. I will rest in the cradle of Your peace forever. Thank you, Lord.

Lord, let Your Spirit lead me to . . .

GOOD MORNING, GOD!
December 6

Isaiah 43:2-3a

When you pass through the waters, I will be with you; and when you pass through the rivers, they will not sweep over you. When you walk through the fire, you will not be burned; the flames will not set you ablaze. For I am the Lord your God, the Holy One of Israel, your Savior.

Good Morning, God! Father God, Your promises become sweeter and sweeter each day. I love being in Your Word and being filled with the joy and hope it brings. How can I possibly allow myself to worry? How explicit do You have to be before I understand and believe? *We can pass through water and walk through fire* and You will be with us and protect us. You truly are *the Lord our God and Savior.* All praise and honor and glory are Yours alone.

Father, help me to remember You are always with me and . . .

GOOD MORNING, GOD!
December 7

Psalm 121:1-4

I lift up my eyes to the hills—where does my help come from? My help comes from the Lord, the Maker of heaven and earth. He will not let your foot slip—he who watches over you will not slumber; indeed, he who watches over Israel will neither slumber nor sleep.

Good Morning, God! O Lord, *where does my help come from?* Why do I even feel compelled to ask that question? I **know** You are the God, *the maker* of *the heaven and earth.* You know what I need before I ask. You are there for me no matter where I am. You love me so much You *watch over me* always. Help me to be mindful of this today. Let me *be still and know that You are God.*

My help comes from the Lord and I will . . .

GOOD MORNING, GOD!
December 8

Isaiah 50:4-5

The Sovereign Lord has given me an instructed tongue, to know the word that sustains the weary. He wakens me morning by morning, wakens my ear to listen like one being taught. The Sovereign Lord has opened my ears, and I have not been rebellious; I have not drawn back.

Good Morning, God! Thank You, Lord, for this new day. Thank you for the opportunity to serve You and worship and praise You. You tell us You have given Spiritual gifts to all Your children. I may not have the gift of eloquent speech, but I can certainly listen and hear all that You have to say to me today. *Waken my ear to listen like one being taught.* Help me to hear Your voice in all I do today and let it be a *light unto my path.* Let me learn Your ways and follow them.

Lord, open my ears so that . . .

GOOD MORNING, GOD!
December 9

Psalm 31:14-16

But I trust in you, O Lord; I say, "You are my God." My times are in your hands; deliver me from my enemies and from those who pursue me. Let your face shine on your servant; save me in your unfailing love.

Good Morning, God! Lord, it just seems that some days everything around me is crumbling. It seems that my enemies are so close I can almost feel their heated breath as they run after me. Lord, *but I trust in you.* Whom or what shall I fear? *You are my God.* You have overcome the world and Satan and all his minions. I am a child of the One True God. *Let your face shine on your servant; save me in your unfailing love.* Praise God!

My times are in your hands, Lord, so use me to . . .

GOOD MORNING, GOD!
December 10

Mark 6:36-37

[Before Jesus fed the 5,000...] *Send the people away so they can go to the surrounding countryside and villages and buy themselves something to eat. But he answered, "You give them something to eat." They said to him, "That would take eight months of a man's wages! Are we to go and spend that much on bread and give it to them to eat?"*

Good Morning, God! Precious Savior, why am I so quick to look to the obvious, practical side of this world instead of seeing through Your eyes. I try to put You in a box of time and space and forget *through You all things are possible.* Help me to see the power of prayer and the power of Your Spirit that lives within me. Help me not to doubt the things I can do through that same power. Let me realize that through Your power there is no limit to what I can do for You and Your children.

Lord, let me see what I can do for You today and . . .

GOOD MORNING, GOD!
December 11

Matthew 6:14-15

For if you forgive men when they sin against you, your heavenly Father will also forgive you. But if you do not forgive men their sins, your Father will not forgive your sins.

Good Morning, God! Forgiveness is a mighty word. It can destroy both the sinner and the one who withholds forgiveness. To not forgive is a bottomless pit of despair and sorrow. One can never be at peace with unforgiveness in their heart. It will constantly torment you and destroy your soul. Lord, help me to feel the forgiveness You have so richly lavished on me, one of the foremost sinners. Your goodness, grace and mercy cover me and I am overjoyed. Thank You, Lord.

Lord, use me to help bring forgiveness and . . .

GOOD MORNING, GOD!
December 12

Jeremiah 10:23-24

I know, O Lord, that a man's life is not his own; it is not for man to direct his steps. Correct me, Lord, but only with justice – not your anger, lest you reduce me to nothing.

Good Morning, God! Father God, as I begin this day, I need You to guide me. I find myself planning my day – what I must do and what I should do. I plan and plan and very seldom do I accomplish what I thought was so important. Help me to begin my day asking you to *direct my paths.* Help me to listen for Your *still, soft voice* to lead me in the way You would have me go. Give me the faith to completely trust You to be in control of my life. It isn't up to me but to You, O Lord. That is so comforting.

Lord, show me the way to . . .

GOOD MORNING, GOD!
December 13

Ruth 1:16-17a

But Ruth replied, "Don't urge me to leave you or to turn back from you. Where you go I will go, and where you stay I will stay. Your people will be my people and your God my God. Where you die I will die, and there I will be buried."

Good Morning, God! What total love and devotion this is. As I read this scripture, I am reminded of the love You have for me. You have showered me with Your love and blessings. My cup overflows. Lord, help me to know You and have such a loving relationship with You that these words express how I care for You. Let me be ready to *go where you go, and stay where You stay.* Let me completely give myself to You and Your plan for my life. My life is for Your glory.

Lord, fill me with Your love and let me share it with . . .

GOOD MORNING, GOD!
December 14

John 4:13-14

Jesus answered, "Everyone who drinks this water will be thirsty again, but whoever drinks the water I give him will never thirst. Indeed, the water I give him will become in him a spring of water welling up to eternal life."

Good Morning, God! It seems that I spend so much of my time and energy running in circles. I think I have a purpose and a destination for You – to do Your work and will, but I don't quite get there. I keep going to the well and coming away empty. Lord, fill me with Your living water. Let it course through my veins and fill me to overflowing. Let Your Spirit completely satiate my entire being and send me forth with Your mission on my heart.

Lord, send me to Your thirsty children so that . . .

GOOD MORNING, GOD!
December 15

Romans 12:10-12

Be devoted to one another in brotherly love. Honor one another above yourselves. Never be lacking in zeal, but keep your spiritual fervor, serving the Lord. Be joyful in hope, patient in affliction, faithful in prayer.

Good Morning, God! I am so filled with Your love today. I feel Your presence and I want to share the beautiful joy I have in You. I want everyone to know You and Your goodness, grace and mercy. Use me as Your vessel of love today. Let me show love where there is hate or sorrow. Let me show love where this is strife and mistrust. Let me show love where there is injustice and unforgiveness. Let me *never be lacking in zeal, but keep spiritual fervor, serving You.*

Lord, my prayer today is . . .

GOOD MORNING, GOD!
December 16

3 John 1:2-4

Dear friend, I pray that you may enjoy good health and that all may go well with you, even as your soul is getting along well. It gave me great joy to have some brothers come and tell about your faithfulness to the truth and how you continue to walk in the truth. I have no greater joy than to hear that my children are walking in the truth.

Good Morning, God! Lord, what a beautiful picture of Godly life. John gave his life to follow You and as he served you, he saved many souls. Teach us to be faithful *and to continue to walk in the truth.* You have blessed us with many wonderful scriptures of how to live the Christian life. My *soul is getting along well* as I spend time with You each day in Your Word and in prayer. It is my greatest joy to be with You each day.

Help me to continue to walk in the truth and . . .

GOOD MORNING, GOD!
December 17

Psalm 84:1-3

How lovely is your dwelling place, O Lord Almighty! My soul yearns, even faints, for the courts of the Lord; my heart and my flesh cry out for the living God. Even the sparrow has found a home, and the swallow a nest for herself, where she may have her young – a place near your altar, O Lord Almighty, my King and my God.

Good Morning, God! O Lord, how I yearn to be in Your *courts.* I begin each day in prayer and long to be so close to You that I can feel You. I know that my joy and peace are in You. I want to stay close to You all throughout the day. I don't want to let the world lead me astray and into the snares of Satan. It is so easy to get caught up in the *Babylon* of this world. Let me find my *nest and resting* place in You, *O Lord Almighty, my King and my God.*

Lord, let me stay *near Your altar* today so that I may . . .

GOOD MORNING, GOD!
December 18

Daniel 2:20-22

Praise be to the name of God for ever and ever; wisdom and power are his. He changes times and seasons; he sets up kings and deposes them. He gives wisdom to the wise and knowledge to the discerning. He reveals deep and hidden things; he knows what lies in darkness and light dwells with him.

Good Morning, God! So often it seems this world is spinning out of control. So many things are acceptable that are against Your Word. It seems that it has become the *norm* for people to believe whatever is convenient for them at the time. You tell us in Your Word that You alone are in control. You *reveal the deep and hidden things.* You know the big picture and You reign! Glory in the highest, You reign.

Lord, let me know that You reign and give me the courage to declare that . . .

GOOD MORNING, GOD!
December 19

Genesis 46:2-4

And God spoke to Israel in a vision at night and said, "Jacob! Jacob!" "Here I am," he replied. "I am God, the God of your father," he said. "Do not be afraid to go down to Egypt, for I will make you into a great nation there. I will go down to Egypt with you, and I will surely bring you back again. And Joseph's own hand will close your eyes."

Good Morning, God! There are so many frightening things in life. I don't know which way to turn. I read the scriptures and I pray but still I am not sure what it is You want me to do. I need to know that You *are God, the God of our father.* I must realize that You *will go with me* wherever You lead. You will make me prosper and show me the way You want me to go. Thank You, Lord. What comfort that is.

Lord, if you lead me to Egypt, I know You will be with me and . . .

GOOD MORNING, GOD!
December 20

Luke 1:34-35

"How will this be," Mary asked the angel, "since I am a virgin?" The angel answered, "The Holy Spirit will come upon you, and the power of the Most High will overshadow you. So the holy one to be born will be called the Son of God. . ."

Good Morning, God! O Lord, what miracles You perform. What glorious gifts You bestow on Your children. You love us so much that You gave Your only Son. A Savior is to be born of a virgin as prophesied hundreds of years prior. Lord, give me the faith of Mary. Let me be found in Your favor. Let Your Holy Spirit work within me to proclaim the Good News to everyone. Use me, Lord. Let Your Spirit burn within me and let me ever praise Your Holy Name!

Lord, let *the power of the Most High overshadow me* in order to . . .

GOOD MORNING, GOD!
December 21

Luke 1:46-49

And Mary said: "My soul glorifies the Lord and my spirit rejoices in God my Savior, for he has been mindful of the humble state of his servant. From now on all generations will call me blessed, for the Mighty One has done great things for me – holy is his name."

Good Morning, God! Father God, let *my soul glorify the Lord and my spirit rejoice in God my Savior.* Let this permeate my soul and my being. Let me comprehend the richness of this incredible gift. Holy Spirit fill my thoughts with what You would have me say and do today to show Your glory. I give You thanks and praise for calling me Your child. I am a child of the *Mighty One.* All praise and glory to You, my Savior King.

Lord, help me to see the magnitude of this blessing and . . .

GOOD MORNING, GOD!
December 22

Isaiah 9:6-7

For to us a child is born, to us a son is given, and the government will be on his shoulders. And he will be called, Wonderful Counselor, Mighty God, Everlasting Father, Prince of Peace. Of the increase of his government and peace there will be no end. He will reign on David's throne and over his kingdom, establishing and upholding it with justice and righteousness from that time on and forever.

Good Morning, God! What an incredible promise, O God. Your Son has come and is the Savior of the world. *Mighty God, Everlasting Father, Prince of Peace.* How magnificent is the Name of the Lord. How glorious are all Your works. I want to share this wonderful story with everyone. This is the reason for the season. Help me to be aware of Your gift as I hurry about trying to create my own idea of Christmas.

Prince of Peace, create a right spirit within me and . . .

GOOD MORNING, GOD!
December 23

Isaiah 44:23

Sing for joy, O heavens, for the Lord has done this; shout aloud, O earth beneath. Burst into song, you mountains, you forests and all your trees, for the Lord has redeemed Jacob, he displays his glory in Israel.

Good Morning, God! This is the season of singing praises to Your Name. I want to *shout aloud and burst into song.* You have *redeemed* the world and have given Your Son. Praise God from Whom all blessings flow. Your plan for our eternity was laid with the foundations of the earth. When You created mankind You knew we would fall away and in Your infinite wisdom and mercy, You provided a Savior for all who believe. I do believe, Lord, and I praise Your Holy Name.

Thank You for the gift of Your Son and . . .

GOOD MORNING, GOD!
December 24

Luke 2:10-12

But the angel said to them, "Do not be afraid. I bring you good news of great joy that will be for all the people. Today in the town of David a Savior has been born to you; he is Christ the Lord. This is the sign to you: You will find a baby wrapped in cloths and lying in a manger."

Good Morning, God! What humble beginnings for a Glorious Savior. What love and mercy to us all in that You continually tell us, *Do not be afraid.* Your unending outpouring of love is overwhelming and so hard to comprehend. Such *good news of great joy!* The Savior has come down from His throne to dwell among men. What kind of love is this that You should make this sacrifice for me? Thank You, Lord Jesus.

Precious Savior, open my heart to . . .

GOOD MORNING, GOD!
December 25

Luke 2:13-14

Suddenly a great company of the heavenly host appeared with the angel, praising God and saying, "Glory to God in the highest, and on earth peace to men on whom his favor rests."

Good Morning, God! O Lord, Your joy and peace abound today above all days. This is the day You gave up Your seat at the right hand of the Father to come to earth for the salvation of all. *Glory to God in the highest.* I will ever praise You and worship You. I pray Your Spirit fills me to overflowing with the Love of Christ for His people. Let me be an earthen vessel which You use to tell others of Your unending love and goodness.

Lord, let *Your favor rest upon me* and show me . . .

GOOD MORNING, GOD!
December 26

2 Corinthians 1:3-4

Praise be to the God and Father of our Lord Jesus Christ, the Father of compassion and the God of all comfort, who comforts us in all our troubles, so that we can comfort those in any trouble with the comfort we ourselves have received from God.

Good Morning, God! You are the God of *compassion and the God of all comfort.* No matter what my circumstance, I know I can turn to You. You are a God of love and understanding. It sometimes seems that the evil one is causing trouble all around me, but I know that my God has overcome Satan and all his evil angels. You are there in my time of trouble and sorrow. You guide me through to Your peace. Help me to show that same love and comfort to *those in any trouble.* Help me to show Your love and mercy to them as You have shown me.

Thank You for Your compassion and . . .

GOOD MORNING, GOD!
December 27

Ephesians 4:1-3

As a prisoner for the Lord, then, I urge you to live a life worthy of the calling you have received. Be completely humble and gentle; be patient, bearing with one another in love. Make every effort to keep the unity of the Spirit through the bond of peace.

Good Morning, God! This is my heart's desire, that I *live a life worthy of the calling I have received* in You. I want to bring gentleness and love to everyone. I pray that You would guide me in Your ways, O Lord – not my life, but Yours. I want to live for You and do Your will and be Your servant. Take my heart and make it all for You. Let me be a source of Your love and peace to all the world. Let your Light shine through me.

Teach me to *be completely humble and gentle* so that . . .

GOOD MORNING, GOD!
December 28

Philippians 4:12-13

I know what it is to be in need, and I know what it is to have plenty. I have learned the secret of being content in any and every situation, whether well fed or hungry, whether living in plenty or in want. I can do everything through him who gives me strength.

Good Morning, God! You are the great Jehovah Jireh, The Lord Will Provide. Even in the darkest of times, I can turn to You for strength and courage to endure. You are always there for me. I praise You that You have instilled in me to trust You in every situation. You reign. *You know the plans You have for me.* In times of trouble I find myself more and more on my knees. You hear my prayers. *I can do everything through him who gives me strength.*

Lord, teach me *the secret of being content in any and every situation* and . . .

GOOD MORNING, GOD!
December 29

1 Thessalonians 5:9-11

For God did not appoint us to suffer wrath but to receive salvation through our Lord Jesus Christ. He died for us so that, whether we are awake or asleep, we may live together with him. Therefore encourage one another and build each other up, just as in fact you are doing.

Good Morning, God! Lord, You have promised us an eternity with You. You have chosen us to a relationship that cannot be broken. We have *received salvation through our Lord Jesus Christ.* What a glorious thought. Help me to live my life worthy of that salvation. Help me to *encourage and build up* the Body of Christ. Give me the words that will help them join in this holy relationship with You.

I surrender my life to You, O Lord. Use me to . . .

GOOD MORNING, GOD!
December 30

Isaiah 42:16

I will lead the blind by ways they have not known, along unfamiliar paths I will guide them; I will turn the darkness into light before them and make the rough places smooth. These are the things I will do; I will not forsake them.

Good Morning, God! At times I feel as if I am blindly stumbling through life without any direction or sense of purpose. I hate these periods of uncertainty because I feel far away from You. How can I let myself be caught in this snare of Satan? He is the father of all lies. I know You are my God and You will be with me always. You promise to *guide me and turn the darkness into light and make the rough places smooth.* Why do I let Satan deceive me? You *will not forsake me.* Thank You, Father God, my Rock and my Redeemer.

I love you, Lord. Let me show You by . . .

GOOD MORNING, GOD!
December 31

Psalm 106:47-48

Save us, Lord our God, and gather us from the nations, that we may give thanks to your holy name and glory in your praise. Praise be to the Lord, the God of Israel, from everlasting to everlasting. Let all the people say, "Amen!" Praise the Lord.

Good Morning, God! I sometimes awaken with a pall of fear covering me. This world is so corrupt and there is so much evil everywhere I'm afraid to get out of bed. I know by battles with the enemy lay ahead. He is *prowling around like a hungry lion seeking whom he may devour.* Lord, I pray that You *gather us from the nations.* Set us apart for You and let us lean only on You for our strength and courage. We are Your people and You are our Father. Let me remember this all day as I raise Your *shield of faith to fight off Satan's arrows.*

Again I say, *Let all the people say, "Amen!" Praise the Lord.*

ABOUT THE AUTHOR

My life had been a normal, every-day life until about 14 years ago. I worked in the secular world for years until I felt God calling me to work for Him.

As this tugging increased, I continued to pray about it and I realized this feeling was real, but what did God have in mind? As I continued to pray, I became certain that God would reveal His will in His time.

I was laid off from my paralegal position and realized it was God's will. I would have never quit that job. Through prayer and daily time spent in His Word God's call became so obvious I could no longer ignore it. I was so excited and just couldn't wait to get to work doing His will, but what was that will? I was sure He had something spectacular in mind for me. You know, like "Mother Ginger" or something like that.

Days, weeks, months and years began to go by and still no word from God. I spent more and more time alone with Him reading His Word with tears streaming down my face beseeching Him to give me a sign – open a door or whatever, but nothing came. I knew He would provide, but what was going on?

I was ready to do His work! I didn't realize I wasn't ready and had not completely given myself to Him -- trusting Him with my future. After much pruning and prayer, He revealed to me His plan for my life.

I am incredibly blessed to be called by God to "Feed His sheep." Writing *Good Morning, God!* is in response to that call. He truly inspired me through the Holy Spirit with the words and thoughts contained herein. He wants a personal relationship with each of us and this book can give us that relationship.

Most of us don't have time to spend alone with Him each day. This devotion of scripture and prayer will open the door to knowing Him better and we will love Him more. I pray that the "dangling prayer" at the end of each day will inspire us to continue praying our heart to the Lord. If we just spend a few minutes each day it can lead to more and more time in His Word and in prayer. Before we know it, we can't let a day go by without spending "quiet time" with Him.

I am a child of God and have been blessed to the point my cup overflows. I love the Lord and want everyone to know Him and love Him. I am the Director of Adult Ministries at Westminster United Methodist Church in Houston, Texas. Among other things, I lead Bible studies and care for our members.

I have been married to one of God's special Angels, Dennis Hurta, for 45 years. He is my soul mate, best friend and love of my life. He is my greatest support and has faith in what God is doing in both of our lives.

We have both been Christians all our life. We went to church but realized we were just "pew warmers." We both attended The Walk to Emmaus in 2002 and our lives were changed. Praise God.

We are blessed to be on our faith journey together and look forward to each new day with anticipation of what God has in store. We know that all things come from God and He is showering us with His blessings, grace and love.

We also know that all things work together for the good for those who love the Lord and are called according to His purpose. We want to spend our life furthering the Kingdom and bringing people to Christ. That is our greatest joy.

I pray *Good Morning, God! will* give you a strong, personal relationship with the Lord and you will be richly blessed by being in His Word and prayer each day. God Bless you.

Printed in the United States
By Bookmasters